A Trip to Palestine and Syria

Also from Westphalia Press
westphaliapress.org

A Trip to
Palestine and Syria

by John P. Hackenbroch

WESTPHALIA PRESS
An imprint of Policy Studies Organization

Westphalia Press
An imprint of Policy Studies Organization
1527 New Hampshire Ave., NW
Washington, D.C. 20036
info@ipsonet.org

ISBN-13: 978-1633910256
ISBN-10: 1633910253

Cover design by Taillefer Long at Illuminated Stories:
www.illuminatedstories.com

Daniel Gutierrez-Sandoval, Executive Director
PSO and Westphalia Press

Devin Proctor, Director of Media and Publications
PSO and Westphalia Press

Updated material and comments on this edition
can be found at the Westphalia Press website:
www.westphaliapress.org

A TRIP TO
PALESTINE AND SYRIA

BY

JOHN P. HACKENBROCH

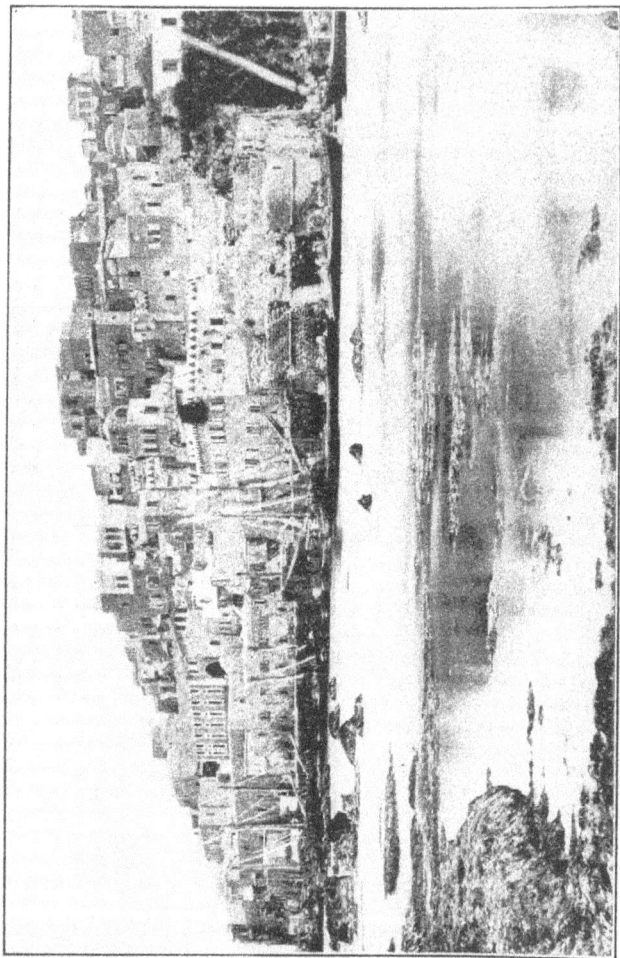

JAFFA.

Preface

This trip to Palestine and Syria was made on a Cook's tour, and, since the firm of Thomas Cook & Son is practically the best of its kind in the world, our party was managed without any of the inconveniences of delay or possible danger.

Our first landing place, according to the program in our guide book, was at Jaffa and from there, under the direction of our conductor, we went to the Holy City of Jerusalem and the sacred places in its vicinity; to Bethlehem, the birthplace of the Saviour; by the Pools of Solomon to Hebron, then to the Dead Sea, the River Jordan, Jericho and Bethany.

Continuing towards the north of Palestine and Syria, we passed through the cities where Jesus had preached—to Samaria, to Nazareth, His home, and by Mount Tabor to the Sea of Galilee and the ancient Capernaum. From there to Damascus, to the ruins of Ba'albek and over Mount Lebanon, and finally we again reached the Mediterranean at Beyrout.

In this volume I have not tried to supply exhaustive information, nor to unravel the multitudinous threads of controversy woven round nearly every sacred spot. I have endeavored to record an interesting journey, to point out interesting spots seen, and to give concise information which may in some measure interest the reader as it did the traveler. The accompanying twenty-

4 PREFACE.

one illustrations must give an added interest to the book itself in their number and beauty, all being reproductions of artistic photographs.

With the kind permission of Thomas Cook & Son, I have frequently referred to the "Tourists' Handbook for Palestine and Syria" and have used it as a foundation on which to build my narrative.

JOHN P. HACKENBROCH,

Paterson, New Jersey.

Contents

PALESTINE AND SYRIA

CONTENTS. 7

CONTENTS.

Illustrations

PAGE

A Trip to Palestine and Syria

Approaching Jaffa from the sea, we were struck with the particular beauty of the scene, while experiencing the strange impression of looking upon the land sacred above any earthly place.

It is the Holy Land, where our Lord Jesus Christ was born, the sacred places where He trod, where He performed so many miracles, where He suffered and died for our sake, and where He, the Saviour of all men, arose from the dead and ascended into Heaven.

It is the Holy Land, the country of Jacob and David, of Rachel and Ruth. Among yon hills the prophets of Israel taught, and the Saviour of all men lived and died.

That stony hillock of a town is the Joppa to which Hiram sent the cedar wood. The roadstead is the port from which Jonah sailed on his stormy voyage. The stretch of sand, relieved here and there by a palm, a fig tree or a pomegranate, is the forepart of that plain of Sharon on which all the roses of imagination bloom and shed their perfume. Yon towering chain of hills was the mountain home of Judah, Benjamin and Ephraim, and with Hebron, Zion, Bethel and Gerizim for its most eminent peaks of sacred memory.

Jaffa, or Jâffe, is the Joppa of Scripture. Some say it was named after Japhet, son of Noah; ancient geographers affirmed that a city existed there before the flood,

13

and others claim the name is derived from *Yafeh*, meaning beautiful. Some classic students liken the name to that of Iopa, daughter of Æolius, and in Jaffa, or Iopa, was laid the scene for the legend of Andromeda—in Pliny's time the chains were still shown with which Andromeda had supposedly been bound to the rocks and left a victim to the cruel monster later slain by Perseus. In Joshua 19.46, it is called Japho; elsewhere in the authorized version it is Joppa. In the Apocrypha it is Joppe (1 Esdras 5.55).

In Biblical history Jaffa is described, in Joshua 19.46, as being in the boundaries of Dan. In Solomon's time, when Hiram, King of Tyre, sent cedar and pine wood for the building of the Temple, he said in his contract: "We will cut wood out of Lebanon, as much as thou shalt need, and we will bring it to thee in floats by sea to Joppa * * * and will cause them to be discharged there" (1 Kings 5.9)—"and thou shalt carry it up to Jerusalem" (2 Chron. 2.16).

The materials for the rebuilding of the Temple under Zerubbabel were also brought "from Lebanon to the sea of Joppa" (Ezra 3.7). Jonah, fleeing "from the presence of the Lord, went down to Joppa, and he found a ship going to Tarshish" (Jonah 1.3). The succeeding circumstances are referred to by our Lord as typical of Himself (Matt. 12.40).

Here the Apostle Peter had that remarkable vision, showing him that the distinction between Jew and Gentile was forever abolished. Here he restored Dorcas to life (Acts 9.31-43), and lodged at the house of one Simon, a tanner, a house to be henceforth memorable in the world's history as the spot where divine command was given to include the Gentiles in the fold of Christ (Acts 10.9-23).

During the stormy period that elapsed between the

last of the prophets and the coming of our Saviour, Joppa was a place of great importance, and was considered a key to the district.

When Pompey invaded Syria, in B. C. 63, Joppa was annexed to that province. It was subsequently part of the possessions of Herod the Great and Archelaus, until, with all Palestine, it became a part of the Roman province of Syria.

Since that day, Joppa has had various revolutions. In the last Jewish War, Josephus states that 80,000 inhabitants were slain by Cestius. For a thousand years it has been the principal landing place for pilgrims going to Jerusalem. During the Crusades, Paynim and Christian took and retook, fortified, destroyed, and rebuilt Joppa as occasion served. After the Crusades, desolation set in, and in the thirteenth century travels the town is described as a mere collection of tents, no habitable house remaining. During succeeding times it again revived, and resumed a portion of its old importance. In 1797 the French took the place, and shot on the strand 4,000 Albanians, who had surrendered after receiving a solemn promise of safety. Here also Napoleon, when obliged to retreat, had 500 sick soldiers poisoned in the plague hospital.

The **House of Simon the Tanner** is still shown, and Dean Stanley considers that circumstances are all in favor of the site having been truly identified. The **town of Jaffa** is beautiful from the sea, but the reverse of beautiful in the midst of its streets, which are dirty, narrow, and winding. The houses are built promiscuously, and, although seeming picturesque from a distance, command no admiration upon a nearer view. Many donkeys and camels we met in the streets, but no vehicles. The population is estimated at from 25,000 up to 30,000 and is increasing. There are about a thousand Christians, a few Jews, and the rest are Mohammedans.

There are three convents at Jaffa—the **Greek Convent,** near the landing place, the **Latin Convent** (the house of Simon the Tanner), and the **Armenian Convent,** where the plague sufferers were poisoned by Napoleon's orders.

There are three mosques in Jaffa, but none of them present any remarkable features.

The most interesting things in Jaffa for the sightseer are the orange groves. They are extensive, easily accessible, and the fruit is delicious; I saw on some of the trees hundreds of ripe, luscious oranges, oval in shape and some measuring from ten to fifteen inches in circumference. Other fruits—lemons, pomegranates, watermelons, etc.—also attain great perfection here. For miles round the scene is one of luxuriant beauty. These orchards, or gardens, are protected by hedges of the prickly cactus. There are, in the vicinity, over 300 of these gardens, differing in size from three or four acres to ten or twelve acres; about a hundred of the gardens have two wells, the remainder only one well each. Oranges are sometimes sold in the streets of Jaffa at the rate of ten or twelve a nickel, and about 8,000,000 are exported annually. They are considered the best in the world; we ate several of them and they had a delicious flavor.

From Jaffa to Jerusalem

Leaving Jaffa, and on our way to Jerusalem, we passed the house and the tomb of Samson, the town where his wife had lived, and the place where he killed hundreds of Philistines with the jawbone of an ass. Samson was the strongest man of his time and once broke the jaw of a lion with his hand, but his strength and his weakness are said to have been in his hair. At a time when the Philistines ruled over the Israelites, he chose a Philistine woman as his wife. Betrayed by her, and captured by men of Judah, he was brought into Lehi to his enemies. Before them all he broke his bonds and seizing the jawbone of an ass killed a thousand men. He later loved Delilah and she, for the consideration of a large sum of silver, promised to deliver him into the hands of the Philistines. After various ruses, she discovered the source of his strength and caused his head to be shorn of its seven locks. The Philistines bound him with fetters of brass, put out his eyes and forced him to work at a mill. In B. C. 1117, during the time of a festival, Samson was brought before the princes and chief nobility of the land to be goaded and sported by them. Knowing his end had come he prayed earnestly for the return of his old strength and grasping the two supporting pillars of the temple, as if for support, broke them, meeting his own death bravely and killing three thousand of the most powerful of the land, more than he had ever killed in actual warfare.

17

"Samson's mangled body was brought up from Gaza by his brethren, and buried on his native hill, between Zorah and Eshtaol" (Judges 16.31).

Descending towards Jerusalem the Russian buildings lay to our left, the valley to the right, in which were a large reservoir and the Upper Pool of Gihon, in Isaiah's time the "upper pool in the Fuller's Field," and before us was the Jaffa Gate through which we entered the Holy City.

JERUSALEM.

Jerusalem

(Formerly the camps of Thomas Cook & Son were located outside the Jaffa Gate, but as travelers generally like to make a long stay in the neighborhood of Jerusalem, and in case of bad weather camp life in one locality is not agreeable, arrangements have been made for travelers to stop at hotels, the best in Jerusalem. The writer was assigned to the Grand New Hotel.

On my second trip to Palestine, when my beloved wife accompanied me, our conductors had the party divided into groups for several hotels, and we were assigned to the Hotel Central. These are two good hotels and both inside the walls of the city, situated near Mount Zion, opposite the Tower of David. Their situation commands the best views of the city—the Mount of Olives, Jordan Valley, the Dead Sea, and Moab Mountains).

The natural situation of the city of Jerusalem, not only conveniently central, but protected by the surrounding ravines, above which it rises like a mountain fortress, doubtless led to its pre-eminence over the other cities of Palestine from the earliest times. It is first heard of, perhaps, as *Salem* (Gen. 14.18), the city of Melchizedek; then as *Jebus,* the stronghold of the Jebusites (Joshua 18.28), and it is probable that the Amorites and Hittites, whose territories adjoined that of the Jebusites, where the city stood, shared its possession. The name of Jebus is mentioned on tablets still existing, written by its Amorite king in the fifteenth century B. C. After ineffectual attempts to dispossess this people, the Benjamites were obliged to leave the stronghold of Mount Zion in their hands, and themselves inhabit only the lower part of the city, until King David and his warriors—all their energies aroused by the over-confident defiance of the Jebusites—captured the citadel, which thenceforth took the name of the "City of David" and Jerusalem became the civil and religious center of the United Kingdom of Israel and Judah. Solomon adorned and fortified it with splendid buildings and strong walls and towers, and erected the Temple on Mount Moriah, where tradition laid the scene of Abraham's sacrifice. Hither the Ark was transferred from Mount Zion, where David had placed it.

In Rehoboam's reign, after the ten tribes had revolted, Jersualem was besieged and plundered by Shishak, King of Egypt. This was the beginning of a long period of losses and suffering, in which the city was involved, both through its constant struggles with the rebelling tribes which constituted the Kingdom of Israel, and its repeated attacks from the great nations whose territories almost surrounded Palestine—Syrians, Assyrians or Chaldeans, and Egyptians. Sacred historians attribute this long siege of misery to the gross idolatry which under many of the kings had usurped the place of Christianity and

worship of the one God who had promised to defend the
city so long as its people remained loyal to Him. After
Jerusalem had been pillaged by Philistines and Arabians
in the reign of Jehoram, by the king of Israel in that
of Amaziah, and the Temple had been despoiled of its
treasures to avert impending disaster, the city was
threatened with utter ruin by the Assyrian army under
Sennacherib. During the siege, and after the miraculous deliverance, Hezekiah fortified and beautified it once
more, and brought the waters of Gihon into it by sub-
terraneous passage. His son, Manasseh, was overcome
by the Assyrians, and carried captive to Babylon. On
his return, however, he also repaired the city, and added
to its defences. Josiah had been slain while warring
against Pharaoh Necho, king of Egypt, while the latter
was on his way to besiege the Assyrian city of Carche-
mish. Necho visited Jerusalem on his return, took King
Jehoahaz to Egypt, and exacted a tribute from the city,
and Nebuchadnezzar, king of Babylon, on his return,
pillaged Jerusalem three times. On the last occasion
the Temple and palaces were burned down, the walls
leveled to the ground, and King Zedekiah and the remaining people (for many had been already taken) were
carried captive to Babylon. This was in the year B. C.
586.

After the return of the Jews from their seventy years'
captivity, the city and Temple were slowly rebuilt, but
not without opposition from the rulers, who represented
the various races in Samaria and the surrounding
regions. These people were jealous of the reviving prosperity of the Jews, and it was only by the dauntless
energy of Ezra, Nehemiah and others, that the work was
at length accomplished.

In the year 332 B. C. the city passed, without a siege,
into the hands of Alexander the Great, who respected

its sacred character, and conferred benefits upon it.
Ptolemy I. Soter, king of Egypt (in 314 B. C.), besieged
it on the Sabbath, when the people, in their reverence
for the day, would not resist, and a large number were
carried into captivity.   Again it was wrested from
Egypt by the Seleucidæ of Syria, and one of them,
Antiochus Epiphanes, desecrated and oppressed it with
such unendurable tyranny, that the insurrection of the
Maccabees broke forth, in 166 B. C., leading to a national revolution and the restoration of the Jews to
independence under the sway of the Asmonean princes.
The Tower of Antonia, at first called Baris, was built
by Simon, brother of Judas, in the early part of the
contest, and afterwards improved by Herod the Great.

In the year B. C. 63, Jerusalem was taken by the
Romans under Pompey, made tributary to Rome, and
part of its fortifications were destroyed.   Crassus again
plundered the Temple, and it also suffered from a Par-
thian army which Antigonus, the rightful heir to the
priesthood, had called in to aid him against Herod, son
of Antipater, whom the Roman influence had raised to
a position of authority.   Herod obtained a decree of the
Senate appointing him king, and by aid of a Roman
army took the city in 37 B. C.   He put his enemies to
death, built a new palace and his splendid Temple, and
otherwise beautified the city (a great part of which had
been destroyed, together with several thousand persons,
by an earthquake, in the year B. C. 31), and enlarged
the Baris, calling it Antonia.   Shortly before the death
of Herod the Saviour was born.

Herod's son, Archelaus, was deposed before he had
reigned long, and Judæa then became a Roman province
within the prefecture of Syria, governed by a procurator,
who resided at Cæsarea, and left Jerusalem to be governed
by its own high priest and Sanhedrin.   Coponius was the

first procurator, and Pontius Pilate was the fifth. The latter built the aqueduct crossing the valley of Hinnom. Shortly after the crucifixion of our Lord, Pilate was deposed from office, because of his tyrannical misgovernment, and Herod Agrippa governed Judæa and Samaria, over which his grandfather, Herod the Great, had ruled. Upon the death of Agrippa, however, his son being too young to reign, a procurator was again appointed, and seven in succession (of whom Antonius Felix and Porcius Festus were the fourth and fifth) aggravated and enraged the Jews by their oppressions. At length the standard of revolt was raised; a success gained over the governor of Syria encouraged the Jews in their resistance, and compelled Titus to bring his legions from Egypt. In the year A. D. 70 occurred the siege and utter destruction of the Holy City, accompanied by scenes of unparalleled horror and suffering; the Jews, though themselves distracted by internal dissensions, remained united in a desperately heroic effort of self-defence up to the last. The slaughter was frightful, and the Temple and whole city were burned down, with the exception of part of Herod's palace and his three towers—Hippicus, Phasælus and Mariamne. A Roman garrison occupied these towers, and the Jews soon began to return and to inhabit the ruins. But upon their raising a rebellion (in 134 A. D.), under Bar-chochebas, against Hadrian, the latter expelled them all, and building palaces, temples, etc., transformed Jerusalem into a Roman city, under the name of Ælia Capitolina. A temple was erected on Mount Moriah to Jupiter Capitolinus.

Constantine transformed the place into a Christian city. Julian gave permission to the Jews to rebuild the Temple, but they could not accomplish it. In the year 614 a vast army under the Persian king, Chosroes II., destroyed the churches, and massacred the Christians. The Emperor Heraclius occupied the city, but in the year 637 it was surrendered to the Caliph Omar, and became a Mohammedan sacred city, the Mosque of Omar taking the place of the Jewish and pagan temples on Mount Moriah. In 688 this mosque was replaced by the beautiful Dome of the Rock, built by 'Abd el Melek, Caliph of Damascus. In 969 Jerusalem fell into the hands of the Egyptians, and in 1077 was won by the Turks, who practised such outrageous barbarities upon Christians that the indignation of all Christendom was roused. The first crusade was organized, and in 1098 a Christian host, commanded by Godfrey de Bouillon, entered Syria. Next year Jerusalem was besieged and captured, the garrison and inhabitants massacred, and the crusaders attained the end of their laborious warfare in the possession of the Holy Sepulchre. Godfrey was elected king of Jerusalem, and was succeeded by his relations until the year 1187, when the reigning king, Guy de Lusignan, was taken prisoner in a desperate battle with Saladin, and the city again fell into the power of Moslems.

Richard I. of England and Philippe Auguste of France, who headed the third crusade, were unable to retake the city, though they appointed nominal kings over it. The last of them, John de Brienne, obtained the aid of his son-in-law, Frederick II. of Germany, against the Moslems and the city was yielded to the emperor, through an agreement with Sultan Melek-ed-din of Egypt in the year 1229, on condition that the ruined walls should not be rebuilt.

In 1240 Jerusalem once more came under Mohammedan rule, being taken by the Sultan of Damascus, but three years later his successor yielded it to the Christians, with other cities, to purchase their assistance in a war which was pending against the Sultan of Egypt. The walls were then rebuilt, and extended on the south to include the Cœnaculum, or present Mosque of David. In the year 1244, a Tartar horde, the Kharezmians, took the city, and treated the inhabitants with great cruelty. Shortly afterwards they were dispersed by the Mohammedans of Syria, and it has been a Moslem city ever since that time. In the year 1517, the place was taken, with the remainder of Syria and Egypt, by the ottoman, Sultan Selim I., and in 1542 its present walls were built by Soliman the Magnificent. Napoleon planned to besiege the city in the year 1799, but was obliged to relinquish the idea. In consequence of a revolt, induced by over-taxation, it was bombarded by the Turks in 1825. In 1831 it submitted to the Pasha of Egypt, Mohammed 'Ali, but by European interference he was deprived of his possessions in Syria, and in 1840 Jerusalem again came under Turkish sway, under the reign of Sultan Abd-el-Mejid. In 1881 the population was suddenly increased by 40,000 Jewish fugitives from Russia.

It may assist the reader to refresh his memory with the story of the fall of Jerusalem, and we do so in the graphic words of the late Archbishop of Canterbury.

The Fall of Jerusalem

"It was now the 13th Abib (March-April, A. D. 70), and the city, even at this time of mortal conflict, was crowded with worshippers who had come from distant countries to adore the God of their fathers in His holy and beautiful house, to which the heart of every Jew turned with longing as his home. * * * As Titus

drew near, he stationed the tenth legion at the foot of
the Mount of Olives. The third or outer wall, erected
by Agrippa, and the suburb, soon fell into his hands.
But more than one tremendous sally of the infuriated
defenders soon taught him the danger of an assault upon
the more ancient precincts of the town. Taking up his
station about a quarter of a mile from the wall, he cast
a trench about the city, and compassed it round and kept
it in on every side. And soon famine began to do its
work more effectually than the sword of the Romans.
All this time the mad party spirit of the defenders made
them war with one another at every moment they could
spare from their warfare with the Romans. Now, two
well known parties of robbers and fanatics, under Eleazer
and John of Giscala, were in the Temple, while another,
under Simon, occupied the upper part of the city. As-
sassins prowled through the streets, and in every house
there was death. Meanwhile famine rages, and the well
known story of Mary of Bethezor fulfilled the most
melancholy page of Old Testament prophecy—'the
tender and delicate woman' of Jeremiah 19.8-9 (cf. Deut.
28.53-57; Lam. 4.10, cf. 2 Kings 6.28), the parallel to
which, in 2 Kings 6.28, is mentioned as the lowest misery in the siege of Samaria. Between the 14th of Abib,
when the siege began, and 1st of Tammuz, it is said that
115,000 bodies had been buried in the city at the public
expense; and the Roman general wept as he saw the
misery, calling heaven to witness that not his enmity,
but the madness of the Jews themselves, was the cause
of these unheard of sufferings. At length, by the latter
weeks of July the Antonia was stormed. The daily
sacrifice had ceased, no hope seemed left, and the defenders of the Temple were exposed to an irresistible
assault from the fortress, which commanded its courts.
But their furious zeal made them defend the holy pre-

cincts inch by inch. Titus himself watched the assault, and urged on his soldiers, but to little purpose. It was not till August (9th of Ab), the day, it was remarked, on which the King of Babylon had destroyed the first Temple, that all was lost. Titus, it was well known, was anxious to save the magnificent building, hallowed by the religious associations of so many centuries; and this may account, in part, for the slow progress of his victory. But on this fatal evening, a soldier, against orders, cast a brand into a small gilded doorway on the north side, and in a few moments the whole Temple was in a blaze. A loud shriek of horror from the defenders announced the catastrophe to Titus, who had retired to rest, intending to begin the assault next morning. Wildly rose the uproar; blazing rafters lighted up the darkness, while all around the crackling of the flames and the crashing of the falling roofs mingled with the shouts of the victors and the death cry of the Jews. Titus rushed forth, and in vain gave orders to stay the great conflagration. His soldiers were in the Holy of Holies; they seized upon the treasures, which were scattered all around; not even Roman discipline could restrain them, and 'the abomination of desolation' took possession of the holy place. When the flames subsided, nothing was left of the Temple but a small portion of the outer cloister.

"Even in this hour of horror the wild fanaticism of the Jews was scarcely quelled. The Messiah had been looked for as a deliverer by many, even in this last extremity. The small remnant of the cloister was now burned by the Roman soldiers, and 6,000 unarmed people, with women and children, were destroyed in it, who had been led up to the Temple shortly before by a false prophet, confident that a great deliverer was at hand. But the actual destruction of the Temple, not one stone left upon another, was a death blow; the spirit of the wildest was

now effectually broken. The upper city (the stronghold of Zion) still, indeed, resisted. There Simon had
been joined by his rival John. Some time was neces-
sarily lost before the Romans could raise their works
against the steep bank of the valley of the Tyropæon.
When they did commence the assault, they found that
the defenders had lost their wonted courage; when, on
the 8th of Elul, the Romans burst, with shouts of triumph, into the last stronghold of their enemies, they
found little but silent streets and houses full of dead
bodies; while John and Simon long baffled all search,
being concealed amidst the ruins and in the subterranean
passages.

"Thus Jerusalem was utterly cast down. A portion of
the western wall and three great towers (**towers of
David, Hippicus and Mariamne**) were left standing to
shelter the Roman soldiers; but all the city, Zion, Akra
and the Temple, was left in a mass of scarcely distinguish-
able ruins.

"The fearful catalogue which Josephus has preserved of
those who lost their lives in the siege and the massacre
which had preceded it in this war, tells us that they
exceeded 1,300,000. And even if this be supposed to be
an exaggeration, no one can read the account of the
horrors of the war, and especially of its last struggle,
without seeing that it well called for that terrific imagery
with which its approach had been announced in our
Lord's prophecy."

The Bible events and allusions in connection with
Jerusalem are so numerous that it is impossible in the
limited space of a handbook to enumerate them. "The
name Jerusalem is used eight hundred and eighteen
times in the Scriptures of the Old and New Testaments"
(Osborn). Moreover, most of the principal events are
still associated by tradition with certain spots which were

pointed out to us, and they will be referred to in the descriptions of those places. No one reading the brief summary of the history of Jerusalem, or the pathetic details of its fall, can help recalling some of those touching voices of prophecy which, like a long wail through the ages, have mourned for Zion. This is the burden of the Old Testament:

"How doth the city sit solitary, that was full of people! how is she become as a widow! she that was great among the nations, and princess among the provinces, how is she become tributary! She weepeth sore in the night, and her tears are on her cheeks. * * * She dwelleth among the heathen, she findeth no rest * * * And from the daughter of Zion all her beauty is departed. * * * Zion spreadeth forth her hands and there is none to comfort her" (Lam. 1. 1, 3, 6).

And this, more pathetic still, is the burden of the New Testament:

"O Jerusalem, Jerusalem, thou that killest the prophets, and stonest them which are sent unto thee, how often would I have gathered thy children together, even as a hen gathereth her chickens under her wings, and ye would not! Behold, your house is left unto you desolate" (Matt. 23.37).

Situation of Jerusalem is described thus: "Jerusalem is builded as a city that is compact together. . . . Peace be within thy walls and prosperity within thy palaces" (Ps. 122, 125). And of Zion is said: "Walk about Zion and go round about her; tell the towers thereof. Mark ye well her bulwarks, consider her palaces; that ye may tell it to the generations following" (Ps. 48.12). Solomon can find no metaphor stronger than "Comely as Jerusalem" (Sol. Song 6.4).

Modern Jerusalem

Most travelers have a feeling of disappointment on first seeing Jerusalem; its size is so much less than our imagination had pictured. Associated as it is with the grandest and most sacred events of history, it is difficult to feel that this little town, around whose walls you may walk in about an hour, is the **Holy City**. And indeed, it is not; for the city whose streets Jesus trod was about a third larger. At that time Zion, a large part of which is now a ploughed field, was covered with palaces; and on every side, where now the husbandman pursues his toil, or desolation reigns, were magnificent structures befitting a great capital.

One is surprised also to find how little remains of the ancient city. The present walls were built in the sixteenth century—only a few courses of stone in them belonged to the ancient walls. Its houses are all new, except that here and there a foundation course indicates an ancient period. The rock crops out in the Temple area, at the Church of the Holy Sepulchre, and on the brow of Mount Zion. But the City of Solomon lies buried under the *débris* of many sieges and captures of Jerusalem, you must dig from thirty to a hundred feet to any traces of it. Jerusalem that was, is "on heaps," "wasted and without inhabitant." Excavations have shown that the foundations of the ancient walls are, in some places, 130 feet below the surface. In digging for the foundation of new buildings, the workmen some-

times dig through a series of buildings, one above another, showing that one city has literally been built upon
the ruins of another; and the present city is standing
upon the accumulated ruins of several preceding ones.

All this throws great doubt on many of the present
sacred places of Jerusalem—the real localities lie buried
far beneath the surface of the present city. But the natural features of the country remain substantially un-
changed. "The mountains round about Jerusalem,"
which were of old her bulwarks, are still there. Here
are Olivet and the brook Kidron, Zion and Moriah.
Kings and prophets and holy men looked on these scenes,
and the feet of the Son of God trod the ground on which
we now walk. Somewhere in the buried city under our
feet He bore His cross; and these hills trembled with the
earthquake's power when He expired.

It is only gradually that the explorer finds out how
much that is ancient—Jewish, Christian and Arab remains—can still be seen within and around the city.

Jerusalem stands on four hills, once separated by deep
valleys, which are now partially filled by the *débris* of
successive destructions of the city. Zion, the most celebrated of these, is on the southwest, rising on its southern declivity 300 feet above the valley of Hinnom, and
on the southeast 500 feet above the Kidron. The Tyropæon sweeps around its northern and eastern sides, separating it from Akra and Moriah. Zion was the old citadel
of the Jebusites, and "the city of David." Mount Moriah
is on the east, separated from Zion by the Tyropæon,
and from Olivet by the deep gorge of the Kidron. This
is much lower than Zion; it was the site of the ancient
Temple, and is now crowned by the Mosque. On the
northeast is Mount Bezetha, a hill higher than Moriah,
which, after the time of Christ, was enclosed within the
walls by Herod Agrippa. Mount Akra lies toward the

northwest. It is separated from Zion by the Tyropæon, and from Bezetha by a broad valley running southward into the Tyropæon, as it sweeps around the foot of Zion. It will be seen, therefore, that the city slopes down from the northwest to the southeast; and standing on the northwest angle of the wall we are at the highest point, from whence Moriah can be seen far below on the southeast, with the Tyropæon on the west of it, running down between it and Zion to the junction of the Kidron and Hinnom. The wall of the city is irregular, conforming to the hills over which it passes, but substantially "the city lieth foursquare." A walk around the outside of the wall commands a view of all the exterior objects of interest.

Jerusalem, which stands on four hills, **Zion, Akra, Moriah and Bezetha,** was once ruled by the wicked King Herod, under Roman control, who shed so much innocent blood, and who killed so many good Christians. Rome, which stands on seven hills, **Palatine, Capitoline, Quirinal, Viminal, Esquiline, Cælian** and **Aventine,** was once under the reign of Emperor Nero, one of the most notoriously wicked characters of history, who, after annihilating so many Christians, forced thousands to seek shelter in the catacombs which extend beneath that city. The harrowing details of that period need not be recounted, they are familiar to the world, besides which it is my purpose to confine myself to those descriptions and items of history which have a more direct bearing on the course of my travels.

Excavations in Jerusalem

The difficulties connected with exploration in Jerusalem are enormous, and it is impossible to sufficiently praise the unparalleled labors of Captains Wilson and Warren, Lieutenant Condor, and others, through whose undaunted courage and untiring effort so many important discoveries have been brought to light.

An accumulation of the rubbish of ages has to be dug through in order to reach the sought-for material, and in one spot, the northeast wall of the Temple, worthless matter lay 125 feet deep. It must be remembered that the Jerusalem of today is built upon the remains of other buried cities.

"One city literally lies heaped upon another. For Jerusalem stood no fewer than **sixteen sieges** from Jebusites and Israelites, Egyptians and Assyrians, Greeks and Romans, Mohammedans and Christians. The last, and twenty-seventh, siege took place in 1244 at the hands of the wild Karezmian hordes, who plundered the city and slaughtered the priests and monks. The explorers have thus to do not with one city, but with many. Jerusalem of our day may be considered the eighth, for even before the time of David there was a city there. The second was the City of Solomon, from B. C. 1000 to B. C. 597, a space of 400 years. The third, that of Nehemiah, which lasted for some 300 years. Then came the magnificent City of Herod; then the Roman city, which grew

upon the ruins Titus had made; it again was followed
by the Mohammedan city; and that by a Christian city;
and now, for six hundred years, the modern city has stood
on the ruins of those that preceded it." So we can well
conceive what good ground the Committee have to write
thus: "Rubbish and *débris* cover every foot of the
ground, save where the rock crops up at intervals. The
rubbish is the wreck of all these cities, piled one above
the other. If we examine it, we have to determine at
every step among the ruins of which city we are standing—Solomon, Nehemiah, Herod, Hadrian, Constantine,
Omar, Godfrey, Saladin, Suleiman—each in turn represents a city. It has been the task of the Fund to dig
down to the rock itself, and lay bare the secrets of each
in succession." (E. Condor Gray.)

Some of the difficulties of excavation work with which
archeologists have to contend are the loose and shifting
quality of the soil, which, being saturated with the sew-
age of ages, is a cause of grave danger to the workmen;
the opposition of the Moslems; interference of the Pasha
and local authorities, and the natural indolence of
Oriental workmen. Yet notwithstanding these obstacles,
the work progresses and the results, which have been
generally satisfactory, will occasionally be referred to in
this description of the city.

Present Size and Aspect of Jerusalem

"The town itself covers an area of more than two
hundred and nine acres, of which thirty-five are occupied by the Haram esh-Sherif; the remaining space is
divided into different quarters: the Christian quarter,

including the part occupied by the Armenians, taking up
the western half; the Mohammedans have the northeast
portion; the Jews the southeast. The whole population
is now about 75,000. The circumference is very nearly
two and a quarter miles."

Jerusalem stands on a bald mountain ridge, surrounded by limestone hills, glaringly white. It is enclosed by **walls** averaging about thirty-five feet in height,
and, although massive in appearance, are far from being
substantial. Around the walls are thirty-four **towers,**
and in the walls are eight **gates,** six open and two closed.
The open gates are:

(1) The **Jaffa Gate,** called by the Arabs *Bâb-el-
'Khalîl*—Gate of Hebron, or "The Friend"—on the west,
leads to Hebron.

(2) The **New Gate,** opened August, 1889, situated in
the northwest portion of the town, between the **Jaffa
Gate** and the **Damascus Gate.**

(3) The **Damascus Gate** called *Bâb-el-Amûd,* or Gate
of the Columns, on the north, between the two ridges
of the city, and leading to Samaria and Damascus.

(4) The **Gate of the Tribes,** *Bâb-el-Asbât,* or, according to the Franks, **St. Stephen's Gate,** the reputed site
of the stoning of Stephen, leading to Olivet and Bethany.

(5) The **Dung Gate,** or the Gate of the Western
Africans, *Bâb-el-Mughâribeh,* leading to Silwân (Siloam).

(6) **Zion Gate,** or Gate of the Prophet David, *Bâb
en-Neby Dâûd,* on the ridge of Zion.

The closed gates are:

(7) The **Golden Gate,** *Bâb-ed Dahâriyeh,* i. e., the
Eternal Gate, in the eastern wall of the Haram.

(8) The **Gate of Herod,** called by the Arab, *Bâb-es-
Zahery,* i. e., the Gate of Flowers, opened occasionally
for the benefit of the soldiers, who drill just outside it.

Streets.—The principal are: "The Street of David,"

leading from the Jaffa Gate to the Haram; "The Street of the Gate of the Column," runs from the Damascus Gate until it is joined by the "Street of the Gate of the Prophet David," under which name it continues to Zion Gate; "Christian Street" runs from the Street of David to the Church of the Holy Sepulchre; the "Via Dolorosa" begins at the Latin Convent and terminates at St. Stephen's Gate.

Population and Religions

The population of Jerusalem is variously stated. Recent estimates give it as at least 75,000.

The **Moslems** are for the greater part natives. There are also a considerable number of dervishes connected with the Haram, and also a colony of Africans.

The **Jews** number about 30,000 and are divided into two sections, the *Sephardim*, of Spanish origin, and the *Ashkenazim*, chiefly of German and Polish origin. The Jews in Jerusalem are mainly sustained by charity, Jews everywhere having sent contributions to their poor brethren of the Holy Land. Many have come hither in piety, and among devout Jews burial at Jerusalem has been looked upon as the great *desideratum*. There is "The Rothschild Hospital," founded in 1855, which has done much good service. Sir Moses Montefiore's mission has been to assist the Jews, not by indiscriminate charity, but by giving them means and scope for labor. In January, 1875, being in the ninety-first year of his age, he resigned his position as president of the Board of Deputies of British Jews, and a testimonial to him having been resolved upon, he requested it might take the form of a scheme for improving the condition of the Jews in Palestine generally, and Jerusalem particularly. About £11,000 only has as yet been contributed to the fund, although a much larger amount was anticipated. The reason for this smallness of contribution was that a rumor went abroad that the scheme was only to continue idle Jews in idleness. Sir Moses Montefiore, at the age of ninety-two, went to Jerusalem, in company with Dr. Löwe, to investigate the real state of the Jewish community. He declares that the people are eager, and physically able, to work; that they have only lacked opportunity, and states that they are "more industrious than many men even in Europe, otherwise none of them would remain alive." He proposes colleges, public schools, houses with plots of ground for cultivation, and proceedings are in progress to purchase land and build houses for this purpose, in and around Jerusalem. It is the younger generations who will derive most benefit from these plans; the habits of the older members of the community are too deep rooted for them to immediately accede to the radical changes proposed. The express object of the "Montefiore Testimonial Fund" is "the encouragement of agriculture and other mechanical employments, among the Jews of Palestine."

There are several institutions already in efficient working order for the Jews in Jerusalem: The House of Industry, Girls' Work School, and like institutions.

The **Greek Church** flourishes in Jerusalem, having at its head the Patriarch of Jerusalem, who resides here, in the convent beside the Church of the Holy Sepulchre. Fourteen sees are subject to him. The Greeks have about twenty monasteries in the neighborhood.

The **Armenians** number about 300. Their patriarch,

who is styled Patriarch of Jerusalem, lives at the monastery near Zion Gate.

The **Copts** have two monasteries, at one of which their bishop resides.

The **Latins** number about 1,800. They have a Monastery, an Industrial School, two Girls' Schools, and a Hospital.

The **Protestants** have but a small, though exceedingly useful, community in Jerusalem. A Mission of Enquiry was instituted in 1820 by the Society for Promoting Christianity among the Jews. Dr. Dalton, the first missionary, came to reside here in 1824. In 1841 the governments of England and Prussia entered into an agreement to establish here a bishopric of the Anglican Church, the diocese to embrace Mesopotamia, Chaldea, Syria, Palestine, Egypt, and Abyssinia. The church is on Mount Zion. In connection with it are two good schools, in and outside the city. The present bishop is Dr. Blyth.

The evangelical work at Jerusalem presents many features of interest. The Krishona of Basle, a kind of lay mission, which seeks to propagate Christianity by means of artisans and tradesmen, whose callings give them ready access to the people, occupies several points in Palestine, has its center at Jerusalem, with branches at Jaffa and Bethlehem. The Deaconesses of Kaiserwerth have opened a real "Good Samaritan" establishment, which is open to every suffering human creature, of whatever faith. An orphanage and several schools are under the care of this noble institution. In connection with the Anglican Church there is a little Arab community, under the direction of a pastor from Alsace, whose chief mission-field is among the Jews.

The **Ophthalmic Hospital,** under the control of the Knights of St. John of Jerusalem, is an excellent institution situated on the Bethlehem road, near Jerusalem.

Health of Jerusalem.—Speaking of the healthfulness of Jerusalem as a place of permanent residence, the late Sir Moses Montefiore, in the narration of his tour (1876), says:

"I had some conversation on the subject of general drainage in Jerusalem with a gentleman of authority; he told me that all the refuse of the city is now carried into the Pool of Bethesda, which, strange to say, I was informed, is close to the house intended for the barracks, and the soldiers now living there appear not to experience the least inconvenience from its vicinity. All the doctors in Jerusalem assured me that the Holy City might be reckoned, on account of the purity of its atmosphere, one of the healthiest of places."

The mean temperature, from 1874 to 1881, was, according to Dr. Chaplin:

	Fahr.		Fahr.
January	48.4°	July	73.8°
February	47.9°	August	76.1°
March	55.7°	September	71.5°
April	58.4°	October	68.6°
May	69.3°	November	59.9°
June	72.8°	December	51.4°

Plan of Description.—As there is no difficulty in finding one's way about in Jerusalem, and the whole city is "compact together," it is considered undesirable to describe certain "walks," especially as it is impossible to make such a division correspond to the various tastes and inclinations of travelers. We shall therefore describe: First, The Church of the Holy Sepulchre; second, the Temple, or Mosque of Omar; third, all the principal places of interest within the city, starting from the Jaffa Gate; fourth, a tour round the outside of the city; fifth, the environs.

The Church of the Holy Sepulchre

[The church is in the Christian quarter, in a street sometimes called Palmer Street.]

No one can approach this spot without reverence. It is the shrine at which millions have worshipped in simple faith, believing that here our Lord was crucified, that here His body lay, that here He revealed Himself after His resurrection. The question, which is now the great question of controversy, is this: The Calvary and Holy Sepulchre stand now in the very heart of the city, far within the present walls. Could the site ever have been *outside* the walls about 30 A. D.? If it was, then this may be the very spot where the cross stood on Calvary, and the Sepulchre may be that which Joseph of Arimathæa gave, "wherein never man lay."

It is a pity to disturb the mind of the traveler on the threshold of such a sacred spot, and we have no intention of giving more than a brief *epitome* of the various sides taken in the controversy. The scriptural account is as follows:

"The bodies of those beasts whose blood is brought into the sanctuary by the High Priest for sin are burned without the camp. Wherefore Jesus also, that He might sanctify the people with His own blood, *suffered without the gate*" (Heb. 13.11-12). He was taken from the Judgment Hall "unto a place called Golgotha, that is to say, a place of a skull" (Matt. 27.33). The place where

40

CHURCH OF THE HOLY SEPULCHRE.

Jesus was crucified was *"nigh unto the city"* (John 19.20), and appears to have been beside some public thoroughfare. "They that *passed by* reviled Him" (Matt. 27.39).

The story of the removal from the cross and the burial in the sepulchre is given thus minutely in St. John's Gospel: "And after this, Joseph of Arimathæa, being a disciple of Jesus, but secretly for fear of the Jews, besought Pilate that he might take away the body of Jesus: and Pilate gave him leave. He came, therefore, and took the body of Jesus. And there came also Nicodemus, which at the first came to Jesus by night, and brought a mixture of myrrh and aloes, about an hundred pound weight. Then took they the body of Jesus, and wound it in linen clothes with the spices, as the manner of Jews is to bury. *Now in the place where He was crucified there was a garden; and in the garden a new sepulchre, wherein was never man yet laid.* There laid they Jesus therefore, because of the Jews' preparation day; *for the sepulchre was nigh at hand"* (John 19.38-42). In the Gospel of St. Mark the additional information is given that they "laid Him in a sepulchre which was hewn out of a rock, and rolled a stone into the door of the sepulchre" (Mark 15.46).

There is no historical evidence that the site of the Holy Sepulchre was determined until the third century, when it appears from Eusebius, that over the sepulchre had been erected a Temple of Venus. In the fourth century, the Empress Helena had a vision, in which she recognized the site, and by means of a miracle discovered the true cross. Constantine thereupon built a group of edifices over the sites, A. D. 326. These were destroyed by the Persians in 614 and rebuilt in 616. In 936 fire partly destroyed the church, and the Moslems inflicted damage to it in 1010. The present church was built by the Crusaders in 1103, to enclose the older chapels rebuilt in 1037-48.

The history of the church has been so often recorded, and is such a lengthened story of vicissitudes, that it is out of the province of this book to enter into it minutely. (See the works of Robinson and De Vogüe, and the Memoirs of the Palestine Survey, with Sir C. Wilson's Survey Memoir.)

In favor of the traditional site of the sepulchre it is urged that an undisputed Hebrew tomb (now said to be that of Nicodemus) exists just west of the Holy Sepulchre itself. But the Rabbis (about 150 A. D.), in the Talmud, inform us that ancient sepulchres were known to be hidden underground within the walls of Jerusalem.

As we enter **The Court,** which is a little lower than the street, we notice first the vendors of rosaries and relics, and a miscellaneous collection of beggars, more or less deformed. If any special service is going on, there is a guard of Turkish soldiers, stationed here to keep the peace between rival sects; if no special service demands that they should be drawn up in the court-yard, armed, they will be seen, as I saw them, in the porch or vestibule of the church.

[The best **Time to Visit** the church is early in the morning. It is generally closed from 10.30 to 3 P. M., but admission can be obtained during those hours on payment of a fee. The morning light is the best for seeing the church.]

Entering by the door on the left of the church—the prmcipal entrance—the first of the many places of interest pointed out in this wonderful building, or series of buildings—is the **Stone of Unction,** where the body of our Lord was laid for anointing, when taken down from the cross. This marble slab is about six feet in

INTERIOR OF THE HOLY SEPULCHRE.

length, elevated slightly above the stone floor. The stone which so many thousand pilgrims kiss, is not the stone which tradition calls the Stone of Unction, that being buried beneath the present slab, which was placed here in 1810. Lamps and large candelabra hang over and surround the stone, and these belong to Armenians, Latins, Greeks and Copts, although this portion of the church is the property of the Armenians.

A few steps to the left is a stone enclosed with a railing. This is the **Station of Mary,** marking the spot where she stood while the body of Jesus was being anointed, or where she stood watching the tomb. A few steps further on, to the right, and we enter the **Rotunda.** The dome is sixty-five feet in diameter, and is decorated with mosaics. It is open at the top like the Pantheon at Rome, and is supported by eighteen piers.

The **Holy Sepulchre** stands in the very center of the Rotunda. It "lies within a small chapel twenty-six feet long by eighteen feet broad, built of the Santa Croce marble. A long, low doorway leads to the sepulchre itself, the western chapel. It is very small, being only six feet by seven feet, or forty-two square feet in area, of which space nineteen square feet are taken up by the marble slab shown as the Tomb of the Lord. The slab is cracked through the center, and much worn by the lips of adoring pilgrims. The chapel, marble cased throughout, so that no rock is anywhere visible, is lit by forty-three lamps, always burning."

The sepulchre has two chambers, one, the vestibule, being the Angel's Chapel, in the center of which is the stone which the angels rolled away from the mouth of the tomb. Then, through a low door, the sepulchre itself is seen; the lamps belong to the different sects, four being the property of the Copts. The reliefs in the wall are, in front, the Greeks'; right, the, Armenians'; left the Catholics'. Every day mass is said here.

Whatever may be the emotions of the traveler, as he enters this most remarkable place in the world, he should at least tarry here awhile to observe, respectfully, the feelings of others; and no one can witness the passionate devotion of pilgrims without emotion.

Coming now into the Rotunda, it will be well to make a tour of all the notable places, and the following order is recommended: Just at the back of the Sepulchre, the west end, is the **Chapel of the Copts,** a very meagre affair, but their property since the. sixteenth century. Near to this is the **Chapel of the Syrians,** beside which is a rocky grotto, with tombs, to see which a candle is necessary. Two of these are said to be the tombs of Nicodemus and Joseph of Arimathæa.

Returning to the Rotunda, we find on the north of the Sepulchre an open court with slabs of marble inlaid, and radiating from a central stone, where Jesus stood when He said to Mary Magdalene, who stood in the marble ring a short distance off: "Woman, why weepest thou?" And she, supposing Him to be the gardener, said unto Him: "Sir, if thou hast borne Him hence, tell me where thou hast laid Him, and I will take Him away" (John 20.15). This spot is the property of the Latins.

Ascending now by three steps to the church of the Latins, we enter the **Chapel of the Apparition,** and in a fourteenth century legend it is asserted that here our Lord appeared to Mary after His resurrection. On the left is a painting of the Last Supper. On the right, an altar, and on it a stick, called the Rod of Moses; by putting one end of the stick into a hole over the altar, a stone is touched called the **Column of the Scourging,** to which Christ was bound when scourged by order of

Pilate. This column was formerly exhibited in the reputed house of Caiaphas.

From the door of the Latin Church, turn to the left into the **Sacristy,** where the sword, spurs, equipment and other memorials of the gallant Godfrey de Bouillon are shown. It is said that his tomb was once here, and also that of his brother Baldwin. The sword is one that was a favorite of Godfrey's, and with which he is said to have split a giant Saracen in twain; it is the same sword with which the Knights of St. John are girt, when invested with that honorable order. Leaving this place, we turn to the left, past several columns and come to an altar under which are two holes in the stone; it is called the **Bonds of Christ.** Near it is a small chamber, called the **Prison of Christ,** where, it is said, He was incarcerated prior to the crucifixion. Continuing a few steps eastward along the aisle, we have, on our left, the **Chapel of Saint Longinus,** the centurion, who said, "Truly this was the Son of God." The stone is pointed out on which it is said he was beheaded for preaching the Gospel. Others say that Longinus was the soldier who pierced the side of Christ with a spear, and when, of the water and blood which flowed from the wound, some fell on his blind eye, its sight was immediately restored and, as a result, Longinus became a good Christian. Near to this chapel is the **Chapel of the Division of the Vestments.** "And when they had crucified Him, they parted His garments, casting lots upon them what every man should take" (Mark 15.24).

Near this chapel is a flight of twenty-nine steps leading down into the **Chapel of Helena,** one of the most interesting of the many buildings of the church, inasmuch as it is where the basilica of Constantine once stood. The massive substructions date from the seventh century, the pointed vaulting from the time of the

Crusades. Here is an altar to **Dimas,** the penitent thief, and another to Helena. Near it, to the right, is a niche in a low wall overlooking the cave below, and called the **Chair of Helena,** said to be the place where she sat when search was being made for the true cross.

Descending thirteen steps more we reach the **Chapel of the Finding of the Cross.** The legend will be remembered of how the Empress was divinely directed to this spot; how she watched the digging until eventually the three crosses, with nails, crown of thorns, superscription, and other relics were found. It was difficult to make sure which of the three was the true cross, and at last a noble lady on the point of death was sent for, and as soon as her body touched the third cross she was immediately cured of her otherwise cureless malady, and thus the identity of the true cross was established. The commemoration of this event is called in the calendar, "The Invention of the Cross," and is celebrated on third of May.

"The Empress Helena had ordered a silver casting in which the Holy Cross was encased, and presented it to the Bishop of Jerusalem; but one piece of it she sent to her son, Emperor Constantine, at Constantinople, and another with a plate with engraved letters of command that Constantine build a church in Rome, which was to be called the Church of the Holy Cross from Jerusalem.

"The Emperor Constantine then had a grand church soon built over the Holy Sepulchre and the Holy Cross. From the consecration and festival of this great church, is the festival called 'Exaltation of the Holy Cross' and celebrated on the fourteenth of September ever since.

"In the commencement of the seventh century the Persians robbed the Holy Cross. The Christians then built several little churches over the holy places, which were destroyed by the Mohammedans, who took Jeru-

salem in the year 636 and ruled it until the year 1099;
then the Crusaders gained the victory and instituted a
Christian kingdom, and they built up the Church of the
Holy Sepulchre much larger than it had been.   They
built a second dome, combined with a large arch (Emperor Arch), and on the left side a bell tower, which is
there to the present day. The inside of this church has
been mostly rebuilt since the terrible fire of 1808."

Continuing through the Church of the Holy Sepulchre, the "Chapel of the Finding of the Cross," which
belongs (left) to the Greeks, and (right) to the Catholics, I saw in a slab a beautiful cross, a bronze statue of
St. Helena and a Latin inscription in the wall.   The
steps we reascended were cut out of the rock, and
sounded hollow; it is supposed that an old cistern lies
beneath.

Returning to the aisle at the head of the steps we
found, at a few feet to the left, the **Chapel of the Crown
of Thorns.**   Here is a grayish column on which tradition says our Lord sat while "the soldiers platted a
crown of thorns, and put it on His head, and they put
on Him a purple robe, and said, Hail, King of the Jews!
and they smote Him with their hands" (John 19.2,3).
A few paces west of this altar is a door on the right,
through which we enter the **Church of the Crusaders** or
Greek Church, larger and more gorgeously decorated
than the chapels of any of the other sects.   Here is the
seat of the Patriarch, and reserved places for other dig-
nitaries of the church, namely: Patriarchs, Archbishops.
Bishops, Archimandrites (directors of convents), Ab-
bots, Archpriests, Priests, Deacons, Under-Deacons,
Chanters, Lecturers, and towards the east is the Chor-
Absis, and a beautiful high altar.   In the center of the
marble pavement is a short column marking the **center
of the earth;** from this spot the earth was procured from

which Adam was made. It was also part of the Garden of Joseph of Arimathæa.

In front of the Greek Church is the Holy Sepulchre. Returning, therefore, to the aisle by the same door through which we entered, and then to the right, we have before us a flight of eighteen steps, which we ascend and arrive at **Calvary.** It is fourteen and a half feet above the level of the chapel of the Holy Sepulchre. "And when they were come to the place, which is called Calvary, there they crucified Him, and the malefactors, one on the right hand, and the other on the left" (Luke 23.33). And one of the malefactors addressed Him, saying, "If Thou be Christ, save Thyself and us. But the other answering scolded him, saying, Dost not thou fear God, seeing thou art in the same condemnation? And we indeed justly; for we receive the due reward of our deeds: but this Man hath done nothing wrong."

As we learn the history and customs of the Holy Land we are better enabled to understand the Parables, and I will now tell what I think is meant by Paradise and some phrases of obscure meaning.

The request made by the thief was favorably received, and Jesus gave His promise that the thief should accompany Him to a place which He called Paradise. According to what He told Nicodemus, it was not possible for such a man to enter His kingdom, for He said, "Except a man be born of water (baptized) and of the spirit (have received the laying of hands which signifies entrance of the Holy Ghost), he cannot enter into the kingdom of God." The thief, then, having never been baptized had not the privilege of entering the Kingdom of God, but Jesus said, "To day shalt thou be with Me in Paradise." We know that the majority of those people who believe implicitly in the Bible are of the opinion that the thief was permitted to enter Heaven and enjoy the presence of God—

but have they correctly interpreted what is written? Let us examine what has been said and see if we cannot find a greater truth.

While suffering the agonies of crucifixion, a conversation was carried on between them, which will serve our purpose in opening up an investigation.

"And he said unto Jesus, Lord, remember me when Thou comest in Thy kingdom. And Jesus said unto him, verily I say unto thee, to day shalt thou be with Me in Paradise."

After the body of Jesus had lain three days in the tomb, the spirit again entered into it, the angels rolled the stone from the mouth of the sepulchre and the resurrected Redeemer of the world came forth, clothed in a mortal body of flesh. **Mary,** who had so devoutly adored the Saviour, had come early to the tomb and, weeping, found that the body of her Master was no longer there. A voice spoke, saying **"Mary,"** and she turned and said unto Him, **"Rabboni,"** which signifies Master, and Jesus cautioned her, saying, **"Touch me not; for I am not yet ascended to My Father: but go to My brethren, and say unto them, I ascend unto My Father, and to My God and to your God."** It thus becomes apparent that during the time that Jesus lay in the tomb His spirit had not been in Heaven, or in the presence of His Father, and this was also probably true of the thief. It must be conceded, therefore, that there is little reason to believe that the thief was saved. Jesus asserted that "To day shalt thou be with Me in Paradise," and upon His return He informed Mary that he had not ascended to His Father. Hence it would seem that Paradise and Heaven are not synonymous and that Paradise is not the ultimate goal of the righteous.

The question naturally arises, Where was Jesus during the three days following His death? Happily, we are not left in doubt, for the Scriptures plainly show the nature of those duties which the spirit of Christ was called upon to perform while His body rested peacefully in the newly-made tomb of Joseph. Peter, to whom Jesus entrusted the keys of the Kingdom of Heaven, and who was first of the twelve Apostles, may safely be accepted as an authority, and by turning to his Epistles we gain this information: "For Christ also hath once suffered for sins, the just for the unjust, that He might bring us to God, being put to death in the flesh, but quickened by the spirit; by which also He went and **Preached unto the Spirits in Prison**" (1 Peter 3.18-19). Here we have an account of what He was doing during the first three days when the spirit was separate from the body. The thief at this time went to a prison world, where he had opportunity to hear Jesus preach the gospel of deliverance in common with other captive spirits, "which sometime were disobedient; when once the long suffering of God waited in the days of Noah" (1 Peter 3.20).

With this clue, the words of Isaiah can be better understood when he, addressing Jesus, said, "that Thou mayest say to the prisoners, Go forth" (Isaiah 49.9), and again he said, "He hath sent me to bind up the broken hearted, to proclaim liberty to the captives, and the opening of the prison to them that are bound" (Isaiah 61.1), also "to open the blind eyes, to bring out the prisoners from the prison, and them that sit in darkness out of the prison house" (Isaiah 42.7).

These words of Isaiah support, and to a certain extent agree with, the words of Peter, relative to Jesus preaching to the "spirits in prison." In the days of the flood, men who had failed to obey the commandments of God, and who had suffered for two thousand long weary years, were but fulfilling the penalty which the Saviour later demanded when He said, "Verily I say unto thee, Thou shalt by no means come out thence till thou hast paid the uttermost farthing" (Matt. 5.26). And of that servant who neither prepared himself nor did according to His will, was said: "But he that knew not, and did commit things worthy of stripes, shall be beaten with few stripes" (Luke 12.47,48). In what agony must these suffering spirits have waited, and with what joy must they have greeted the long-expected Redeemer, when He appeared and preached to them glad tidings of an Everlasting Gospel! Through its means alone might they hope to be delivered from the prison so long guarded by Lucifer, son of the morning, who is forever set apart from all others and who "made the earth to tremble and did shake kingdoms; that made the world as a wilderness and destroyed the cities thereof; that opened not the house of his prisoners" (Isaiah 14.16,17).

How grand and glorious is the plan of salvation that the Creator has ordained for His children, reaching from eternity to eternity, covering in its details every possible emergency; controlling, guiding and directing their footsteps while in a pre-existing state; teaching them while sojourners upon the earth, and extending beyond the grave into the spirit world, there to cause their hearts to rejoice and gladden under its kind influence, growing and increasing in might and majesty, power and glory, as the ages roll by, until the inspired words of our divine Master shall be fulfilled: **"Every knee shall bow and every tongue confess."**

Well might Jesus say to the Apostles just previous to His death: "Verily, verily, I say unto you, the hour is coming, and now is, when the dead shall hear the voice of the Son of God; and they that hear shall live. * * * Marvel not at this; for the hour is coming in the which all that are in the graves shall hear His voice" (John 5.25-28). Turning again to the epistle of Peter, we find

this assertion: "Who shall give account to Him that is
ready to judge the quick and the dead. For this cause
was the gospel preached also to them that are dead, that
they might be judged according to men in the flesh, but
live according to God in the spirit" (1 Peter 4.5,6).

Jesus upon one occasion, when explaining the Gospel
to the Apostles, said, "Whosoever speaketh a word
against the Son of Man it shall be forgiven him, but
whosoever speaketh against the Holy Ghost, it shall not
be forgiven him, neither in this world, neither in the
world to come" (Matt. 12.32).

Within the Church of the Holy Sepulchre, at the eastern end of Calvary, is an altar, under which is a hole
through a marble slab to the solid rock. This was where
the Cross of our Saviour was planted; two other holes,
or sockets, right and left, are pointed out as the places of
the crosses for the two thieves. Visitors are permitted to
put their hands into these sockets. This is called not
only Calvary, but the **Chapel of Golgotha**—*Golgotha* sig-
nifying in Hebrew a skull—and a curious tradition affirms
that Adam was buried here. "The legend has more poetry
in it, than many, for one cannot but think that the **idea**
in it is, that the blood of the atonement was destined to
fall upon the head of the first transgressor." Near the
altar, to the right, is a long brass cover over a **Rent in
the Rock,** said to have been made at the time of the
Crucifixion. "The earth did quake, and the rocks rent,
and the graves were opened; and many bodies of the
saints which slept, arose" (Matt. 27.51,52).

A little farther to the right is an altar with a picture
of the Virgin, set in diamonds. All the adornments of
this place are of the richest and most profuse description.
It is a question of **taste** whether, supposing this really is
the actual Calvary, it would not have been a thousand
times better to have left it as the bare rock in the Temple

has been left, strikingly significant in the beauty of its simplicity. To the south is a small chapel which we saw through a window. It is the **Chapel of St. Mary,** said to be the spot where the Mother of our Lord, and the beloved disciple, stood at the time of the Crucifixion, when one of the most touchingly pathetic incidents in the Gospel history occurred: "Now there stood by the cross of Jesus his mother, and his mother's sister, Mary the wife of Cleophas, and Mary Magdalene. When Jesus therefore saw His mother, and the disciple standing by, whom He loved, He saith unto His mother, Woman, behold thy son! Then saith He to the disciple, Behold thy mother! And from that hour that disciple took her unto his own home" (John 19.25-27).

Opposite this window, on a column in the center of the chapel, is a good painting of the Virgin and the Holy Child.

Descending now the stairs at the southwest end near the great door of the church, we turn to the right and enter a chapel under the **Chapel of the Crucifixion,** where used to be the **Tombs of Godfrey de Bouillon and Baldwin I.** In the eastern end there is an altar standing over —it is alleged—the **Tomb of Melchizedek.** The **Rent in the Rock,** which we saw in the Chapel of Golgotha, could also be seen from here by moving the brass which covers it.

In order to visit the **Church of the Armenians** from this chapel, we turn to the west a few paces, past the Stone of Unction, and behind the Station of Mary is a flight of steps leading up to the small church, divided by pillars into three chapels or compartments.

The Church of the Holy Sepulchre is the joint property of the Greeks (who have the lion's share), the Catholics, Armenians and Copts. Each of the sects takes its turn making processions to all the holy places, and worshipping at the sacred shrines. Here are hundreds of beautiful golden and silver lamps different in form and design, hanging from the ceiling at different heights, and many of these burn constantly. "Some of those very large lamps are of solid gold," said one of the Franciscan monks, "they are gifts from princes, princesses and kings, and they burn only on a great holy day or for some special service."

On Easter Sunday afternoon our party went to the Church of the Holy Sepulchre to attend the special service held on that day. The number of Turkish guards had been doubled to insure the preservation of order between sight-seers and worshippers and to keep a road clear for the expected procession, which, when it did appear, proved to be a magnificent spectacle.

The traveler is recommended to visit the Church of the Holy Sepulchre as often as possible while he remains in the neighborhood. Some religious ceremony or festival is generally in progress and, no matter what may be his religious persuasion, some sense of awe and reverence must be inspired by the sight of these devout worshippers, pilgrims of many lands, who have wended a toilsome way toward these holy places.

It is certain that this place, the site of the Crucifixion and of the Holy Sepulchre, shall never be forgotten. During the first century Jacob, younger Bishop of Jerusalem, his mother, and many others were living, who had witnessed the death and entombment of our Saviour, and who could testify to the location of the hallowed ground on which these deeds had been enacted. Then, the Evangelist John, who was living in the second century, brought the facts to a younger generation and through the fervor of his preaching brought many new Christians within the fold of the Church.

In the second century there occurred an uprising of

the Jews against the Roman Emperor Hadrian, under
Bar-Kochba 135 a chr., and Hadrian, who believed the
Christians and Jews to be but different sects of the same
religion, reviled the true church and showed his con-
tempt for it in many barbarous ways.   Finally, after
great persecution of the people, Christians and Jews
alike, the city of Jerusalem was razed, a new city built
upon the ruins, and above Golgotha and the Sepulchre
earth was heaped, paving stones laid and a monument
erected to the Goddess Venus.   The location was
marked, however, by Eusebius the scribe, and he said
that in the year 315 there were many processions of
pilgrims who came to visit the holy places. Hironymus,
at the end of the fourth century, said that so many
bishops, teachers and martyrs had visited the same
places, since the ascension of Christ, that he could not
doubt that their knowledge was accurate.

In the year 313 A. D. Emperor Constantine publicly
acknowledged the Christian religion and he with his
mother, St. Helena, made a journey from Constantinople
to Jerusalem. They restored the site, and the Empress
ordered the building of churches at Bethlehem and on
the Mount of Olives, also the Chapel of the Finding of
the Cross (see page 46) which is now within the Church
of the Holy Sepulchre.

The Church of the Holy Sepulchre, which is built from
the east towards the west, is 100-120 steps long, 60-70
steps wide, and the whole covers a space of between two
and three acres.

The Temple

Where once stood the Temple designed by King
David and executed by Solomon, rebuilt and restored by
Zerubbabel and Herod, is now the **Mosque of Omar,**
called also the "Dome of the Rock," or Kubbet es-Sukhrah. It occupies a part of the spacious area known as
the Haram esh-Sherif; "The Noble Sanctuary."

It is needless to say that nearly every inch of ground
in this sacred enclosure, and almost every stone upon
it, has been the subject of controversy. Many important
points in the controversies have been recently cleared up,
through the indefatigable efforts of the members of the
Exploration Fund, and no doubt—now that so many
scientific travelers visit the Holy Land, and the restric-
tions upon visiting the holy places of the Moslems are
gradually being relaxed—more light will be shed from
time to time on the vexed questions which have arisen,
for the most part, from mere surmises.

Without giving an *epitome* of the questions at issue,
the various arguments of those who have brought much
learning and research to the study and identification of
the holy places, will be referred to as the description
proceeds.

The Mosque of Omar stands upon the summit of
Mount Moriah; tradition says upon the very spot where
Ornan had his threshing-floor; where Abraham offered
up Isaac; where David interceded for the plague-stricken
people, and where the Jewish Temple, the glory of Israel,
stood. No one can stand before this magnificent building, with its many colored marbles glistening in the

sunlight, as once the "goodly stones of the Temple"
shone before the eyes of the disciples, and not be moved
with a strong emotion. One's thoughts rush away to
the past when psalmists wrote, and patriots sung, of
the Temple's glory. Hither the tribes came up; here
shone forth the light of the Shekinah; here was the center of the religious, the poetical, and the political life of
God's chosen nation. And then one thinks of the defeats
and disasters consequent upon disobedience; how glory
after glory vanished, until alien powers desolated and
utterly destroyed the holy place. One thinks of devout
Jews in every land, oppressed and burdened, turning
towards this sacred site, and remembering it with tears
as they pray for restoration to their land. Above all, the
Christian thinks of the little Holy Child presented there
by the Holy Mother, of the Youth asking and answering
questions; and of the divine Man, "teaching and preaching the things concerning Himself."

These, and not the controversial points, will probably
be the kinds of thought in which the traveler will in-
dulge as he stands for the first time within the precincts
of the Haram.

[There is now no difficulty in obtaining admittance to
the Mosque except on great festivals. Application
should be made to the Consul, who will send a kawass.
The fees for admission are regulated by the size of the
party, and it is a saving in expense to join, or form, a
party.]

The Haram esh-Sherif is surrounded by a wall 1,601
feet long on the west, 1,530 on the east, 1,024 on the
north, and 922 on the south, and is entered by seven
gates on the west, the principal being the *Bâb-es Silsileh,*
or the **Gate of the Chain.**

Entering by this gate we have on the right hand the
Mosque-el-Aksa, and before us are steps leading up to

the **Dome of the Rock,** or *Kubbet es-Sukhrah.* The building has eight sides, each sixty-eight feet long, and the
whole covered with richly colored porcelain tiles, and a
frieze of tiles running round the whole building upon
which are written passages from the Koran. There are
four gates, or portals, facing the cardinal points of the
compass.

Tradition states that when Caliph Omar took Jerusalem his first inquiry was for the site of the Jewish
Temple. He was conducted to this spot, then an enormous mound of filth and rubbish, and here he built the
mosque which bears his name. Others claim that the
present mosque was built by Abd-el-Melek in A. D. 686

The **interior** is gloomy, and sometimes so dark that
one has to wait until the eye grows accustomed to it.
The interior has two cloisters, separated by an eight-
sided course of piers and columns; within this, again
another circle of four great piers and twelve Corinthian
columns, which support the great dome. The fifty-six
stained glass **windows** are of great brilliancy and beauty.
The **walls** are covered with tiles, on which are inscribed
portions of the Koran, as on the outer walls of the building. The **Dome** is ninety-eight feet high and sixty-six
in diameter, and is composed of wood. The **pavement**
is of marble mosaic. It was restored by Saladin in
1189 A. D.

There are many things to see in this building, but all
pale before the **Sacred Rock** immediately beneath the
Dome; it is a bare, rugged, unhewn piece of rock about
sixty feet long and forty-five wide. "The rock," says
Captain Wilson, "stands about four feet nine and a half
inches above the marble pavement at its highest point,
and one foot at its lowest; it is one of the 'missæ'
strata, and has a dip of twelve degrees in a direction of
eighty-five degrees east of north. The surface of the

rock bears the marks of hard treatment and rough chisel-
ling; on the western side it is cut down in three steps,
and on the northern side in an irregular shape, the object
of which could not be discovered. Near, and a little to
the east of the door leading to the chamber below, are
a number of small rectangular holes cut in the rock, as
if to receive the foot of a railing or screen, and at the
same place is a circular opening communicating with
the cave."

A hundred **Legends** hang about the rock, Jewish,
Christian, and Moslem. Here, according to the Jews,
Melchizedek offered sacrifice, Abraham brought his son
as an offering, and the Ark of the Covenant stood; on
this rock was written the unutterable name of God,
which only Jesus could pronounce. Some claim that the
Circular Hole is the place through which the blood of
the sacrifices poured, and was carried by way of the
Brook Kidron outside the city. And the Moslems have
strung together some of the wildest and most absurd
of the many legends in connection with it.

The Mohammedan legend of the rock is that when
Mohammed ascended to heaven from here, on his good
steed El-Burak, the rock wanted to follow, and started
for that purpose, but was held down by the Angel
Gabriel, the prints of whose fingers in the rock are still
shown. Ever since then the rock, according to the same
authorities, has been suspended in the air, and the hol-
low-sounding wall is one that was placed there because
pilgrims who passed under the suspended rock feared
lest it should fall and crush them!

The next building of importance in the Haram is
the

Mosque El-Aksa

There is some doubt as to the origin of this building, or group of buildings, but it is generally supposed to be identical (in site, at least) with the magnificent Basilica founded by the Emperor Justinian in honor of the Virgin. De Vogüe affirms that the present structure is entirely Arabian, but its form of a basilica, its cruxiform plan, and the existence of certain ancient remains, prove that it was a Christian church, and has been converted into a mosque. Others, led by Mr. Fergusson, deny that it ever was a Christian church, or that Justinian had anything to do with it, and affirm that it was built by Caliph Abd-el-Mekel, in the end of the seventh century. The Porch has seven arcades leading into the seven aisles of the Basilica. Captain Wilson has so minutely described the interior of the mosque, that we quote his words:

"The porch in front, from two niches for statues still remaining in it, would appear to be the work of the Templars when they occupied the building. In the interior four styles of capitals were noticed; those on the thick stunted columns forming the center aisle, which are heavy, and of bad design; those of the columns under the dome, which are of the Corinthian order, and similar to the ones in the 'Dome of the Rock'; those on the pillars forming the western boundary of the women's mosque which are of the same character as the heavy basket-shaped capitals seen in the Chapel of Helena; and

those of the columns to the east and west of the dome,
which are of the basket shape, but smaller and better
proportioned than the others. One of the small basket
capitals was broken, and, on examination, proved to be
made of plaster; the others of the same series seemed to
be of similar construction, whilst the Corinthian ones
were all of white marble. * * * The columns and
piers of the mosque are connected by a rude architrave,
which consists of beams of roughly-squared timber, in-
closed in a casing of one-inch stuff, on which the decoration, such as it is, is made; the beams are much decayed,
and appear older than the casing. All the arches are
painted. Some of the **windows** in El Aksa are very good,
but hardly equal to those in the 'Dome of the Rock.'
* * * A great part of El Aksa is covered with white-
wash, but the interior of the dome, and the portion immediately under it, is richly decorated with mosaic work
and marble casing. The arabesques and mosaics are similar in character, though of different design, to those of
the 'Dome of the Rock.' During the restorations made
in the present century some paintings of a very poor
order were introduced."

The principal objects of interest in the mosque are:

The **Tombs of the Sons of Aaron**; a stone slab in the
pavement near the entrance. It probably marks the resting place of some distinguished Knight Templar. The
Pulpit at the southern end is exquisitely carved in wood,
and is inlaid with ivory and mother-of-pearl. It was
made at Damascus by a native of Aleppo, and was
brought here by Saladin. The wood is cedar of Lebanon, and the work was ordered by Nûreddin. Near
the pulpit (west) is the **Praying-place of Moses**; and at
the back of the pulpit, is a stone which is said to bear
the imprint of the **footstep of Christ**. Close by here are
two pillars, tolerably close together—so close, that only

medium sized people can pass between them. But every pilgrim is supposed to try; those who succeed are sure of a place in heaven; but for those who fail the case is doubtful! In the eastern end of the mosque is the so-called **Mosque of Omar,** a tradition affirming that he prayed there when he first entered the city.

In the Mosque there is a cistern called the **Well of the Leaf,** the water of which is pure and bright. A curious Moslem legend attaches to this well. It is said that Mohammed delivered a prophecy that one of his followers should, while alive, enter Paradise. During the caliphate of **Omar,** a worshipper, one Sheikh ibn Hayian, came to this well to draw water, when his bucket slipped from his hands and fell in. He went down after it, and, to his infinite surprise, came to a door, which he thrust open, and found it led into a beautiful garden. He wandered about in it for some time, and then returned, but not until he had plucked a leaf, which he brought with him for a token. The leaf never withered, and the words of the prophet were fulfilled; but the door has never since been found. Devout Moslems still look upon the Well of the Leaf as one of the entrances to Paradise.

Leaving the Mosque by the eastern door (at which place the boots of the visitors will be taken by an attendant), we proceed to the southeastern corner of the Haram and descend by thirty-two steps to the so-called **Cradle of Christ,** a small vaulted chamber to which many legends attach. It was here the infant Saviour was brought to be circumcised; here dwelt Simeon; here the Virgin was entertained for some days as his guest, etc. "There," said the guide, "is the altar of Zecharias." From this room we descend to **Solomon's Stables,** a vast succession of pillared and vaulted avenues, bearing, as some suppose, all the marks of the builders of the first Temple; the beveled stones corresponding with the sculptured representations of the stones used in the construction of Solomon's Temple. Here, better than anywhere else, will be seen how the valleys were leveled up to make the vast platform for the Temple. Whether King Solomon's stables were here or not cannot now be ascertained. It is stated 1 Kings 4. 26, "Solomon had forty thousand stalls of horses for his chariots"; and there can be no doubt his palace must have been somewhere close to this place, which was used as stables by the Knights Templars. I saw the rings to which their horses were attached.

Returning to the Haram, and proceeding along by the east wall, we came to a stairway, and, ascending the wall, we got a remarkably fine view. Below is the **Valley of Jehoshaphat,** a mass of graves and memorial stones— the dead of all generations filling up the valley. It is the wish of all devout Jews to be buried here, for to this place will the Messiah come when the prophecy of Joel is fulfilled (3.2): "I will gather all nations, and will bring them down into the valley of Jehoshaphat, and will plead with them there for my people and for my heritage Israel, whom they have scattered among the nations, and parted my land." "Let the heathen be wakened and come up to the valley of Jehoshaphat, for there will I sit to judge all the heathen round about." A good view is obtained of the Kidron, Absalom's Pillar, the tombs of St. James and Zechariah, the Mount of Olives, Garden of Gethsemane, etc.

A little to the north is the **Golden Gate,** or, according to tradition, the "Beautiful Gate" of the Temple, where Peter and John cured the lame man (Acts 3.1-11). There is, however, much more reason to suppose that it corresponds with the Gate Shushan, referred to in the Talmud. If so, "on it was portrayed the city Shushan. Through it one could see the High Priest who burned

the heifer, and his assistants going out to the Mount of
Olives." There appear to have been steps on arches
leading down from this gate into the Kidron towards the
east, and leading up again past the southern end of the
present Garden of Gethsemane. It was through this
gate, according to tradition, that our Saviour entered
Jerusalem on Palm Sunday. It is now walled up, a tradition being extant that, when the Saviour returns to
earth a second time, it will be through this gate He will
make His triumphant entry into Jerusalem, and wrest it
from the Moslems.

Continuing by the east wall I saw a small Mosque,
called The Throne of Solomon. It was here, says an old
legend, that King Solomon was found dead. Looking west-
ward, near the northern wall, is a small chapel, with a
white dome, marking the spot where Solomon gave
thanks upon the completion of the Temple. By going
out of the gate at the northeast corner of the Haram,
about half way between it and St. Stephen's Gate can
be seen through a breach in the wall the traditional Pool
of Bethesda.

Various Prayer Niches are to be seen, to which marvelous legends are attached, and the foundations of a wall
probably belonging to the Fortress of Antonia. The
most beautiful structure in all Jerusalem is probably the
Kubbet es Silsileh, or Dome of the Chain, said to have
been the model for the Mosque of Omar. It is also called
the Tribunal or "Court" of David. The tradition attached to it is that a chain was suspended from heaven
and stood on this spot, and when two disputants could
not settle a quarrel, the chain moved towards the one
who had the right on his side, and so the litigation would
be settled. Another tradition is that every witness in a
great trial was brought here. If he could grasp the chain
his evidence was true; if a link broke off, he was a per-

jurer. The **Kubbet-el-Miraj,** or Dome of Ascension, marks the spot where Mohammed ascended on his wonderful journey to heaven.

One very interesting spot between the Dome of the Rock and El Aksa is a **marble fountain,** called *El Kas,* or The Cup, beneath which are vast reservoirs, and into them the water from the Pools of Solomon was conveyed. These reservoirs and the staircase by which they are approached are all hewn out of the solid rock. Was it here that Solomon placed the Brazen Laver? The cisterns are called the *Cisterns of the Sea, or the King's Cisterns.* Solomon "made a molten *sea,* of ten cubits from brim to brim, round in compass, and four cubits the height thereof. * * * And the thickness of it was a hand breadth, and the brim of it like the work of a brim of a cup. * * * and it received and held three thousand baths" (2 Chron. 4.1-5).

Within the City

Start from the Jaffa Gate for Bab-el-Khulil (i. e., The Gate of Hebron, or the Friend). Jaffa Gate is on the west side of the city, close to the northwestern angle of the citadel. It is a massive, square tower, the entrance from without on the northern side, and the exit from within on the eastern. Entering Jerusalem by this gate a large open space is reached. On the left is a line of shops, *cafés,* etc., and on the right is the **Tower of David,** called by Josephus the Tower of Hippicus, and forming part of the citadel, a strong and conspicuous structure. The upper part of this tower has often been rebuilt, but the town is evidently ancient, the stones being of

immense size, and beveled after the style of the Jews.
At this place David erected a fortress which was the
stronghold of Zion in all after ages, and it is probable
that these immense stones belong to the earliest period
of its history, and may have been laid by him. If it is the
Tower of David, or the Tower of Hippicus built by
Herod, or both, it was standing at the time when our
Saviour was a visitor in Jerusalem, and His shadow may
have rested upon it as He walked in Zion. Josephus
says that Titus, when he destroyed Jerusalem, left standing the three towers built by Herod—Hippicus, Phasælis
and Mariamne. Phasælis and Mariamne have since
been destroyed; only the Tower of Hippicus remains,
from the top of which a splendid view of the surrounding
country may be had, and it is regarded as one of the most
interesting places in Jerusalem. "There is not one house
standing on which we can feel certain that our Lord
ever gazed, unless it be the old Tower at the Jaffa Gate."
(MacLeod.)

Zion Street passes by the east side of the tower, running north and south. We follow it south to the **Gate of
David,** or **Zion Gate,** on the summit of the ridge of Zion.
This height was held by the Jebusites until David took
it by storm, and "David dwelt in the Fort, and called it
the City of David" (2 Sam. 5.9). It was the highest
point within the limits of the city, being 2,540 feet above
the Mediterranean. Here, or hereabout, David's house
was built, the household for his families located, and
here was placed the Ark of God before they built the
Temple. "And David made him houses in the City of
David, and prepared a place for the Ark of God, and
pitched for it a tent" (1 Chron. 15.1,29; 2 Chron. 5.2,
etc.). Opposite the gate is the **Armenian Convent,** one
of the richest and largest in the city, with several large
tamarisk trees in front, said to have been planted by

Herod. Within the convent is the **Church of St. James,** the place where, according to tradition, St. James was beheaded. "Herod the King stretched forth his hands to vex certain of the church, and he killed James, the brother of John, with the sword" (Acts 12.2). The convent is capable of accommodating about 3,000 people. The monks are industrious and are adepts in all kinds of trade. They have in the convent a printing press, a photographic establishment, carpenters' shop, etc.

On Mount Zion, where the palaces of David and Solomon stood, the German Emperor obtained in 1898 for 25,000 reichmarks (or six thousand dollars) a magnificent block of land, and presented it to the German Catholics, and they are erecting a great convent.

A short distance from the church of the Holy Sepulchre is a German church, Die **Erloesungs Kirche** (or **Church of the Redeemer),** built by the gift of the German emperor. His grandmother, Empress Augusta, had purchased the land on which the church is built and it was completed in the year 1898, at the time the emperor was in Jerusalem.

Just outside Zion Gate is a modern ruin called the **Palace of Caiaphas.** It contains the tombs of the Armenian patriarchs. According to tradition, the prison of Christ is here, and the stone which was rolled away from the mouth of the sepulchre (see page 43). It is also the place where Peter stood when he denied the Lord; and a small pillar was pointed out on which the cock stood when he crew to warn him!

A little south of this ruin is a small mosque, known as *Neby Dâûd,* or the **Tomb of David.** It cannot well be doubted that this memorial marks the place, or at least the vicinity of the place, where the Hebrew kings were buried. That they were interred on Mount Zion is known with certainty, for it is said of the successive kings of

Judah, "they slept with their fathers, and were buried
in the City of David," which is only another expression
for Mount Zion (see, 1 Kings 11.43, 14.31, 15.18, etc.).
The notice in Nehemiah 3.16 represents the sepulchre
of David as opposite a certain pool, and the present tomb
stands exactly against the Lower Gihon, on the west of
Jerusalem. The Apostle Peter speaks of the place of
David's burial as a matter of general notoriety. "His
sepulchre," he says, "is with us unto this day." No
reason can be assigned why the locality in that age
should have become a different one from that which
Nehemiah mentions. Josephus furnishes testimony to
the same effect. From that time to the present, as often
as we hear any Jewish witnesses on the subject, we find
them connecting the national tradition respecting David's
tomb with this spot, and the Mohammedans and Eastern
Christians regard it with the same veneration (Hackett).

Learned travelers have, however, placed the Tomb of
David in various other places, within and without the
walls. In the fifteenth century, Benjamin of Tudela
gave this legend:

"Fifteen years ago, one of the walls of the place of
worship on Mount Zion fell down, which the Patriarch
ordered the priest to repair. He commanded to take
stones from the original wall of Zion, and to employ them
for that purpose, which command was obeyed. Two
laborers who were engaged in digging stones from the
very foundation of the walls of Zion, happened to meet
with one which formed the mouth of a cavern. They
agreed to enter the cave, and to search for treasure, and
in pursuit of this object they penetrated to a large hall
supported by pillars of marble, encrusted with gold and
silver, before which stood a table with a golden sceptre
and crown. This was the sepulchre of David, King of
Israel, to the left of which they saw that of Solomon,

and of all the Kings of Judah who were buried there.
They further saw locked chests, and desired to enter the
hall to examine them, but a blast of wind, like a storm,
issued forth from the mouth of the cavern, and prostrated
them almost lifeless upon the ground.   They lay in this
state until evening, when they heard a voice commanding
them to rise and go forth from the place.   They proceeded, terror-stricken, to the Patriarch, and informed
him of what had occurred.   He summoned Rabbi Abra-
ham-el-Constantine, a pious ascetic, one of the mourners
of the downfall of Jerusalem, and caused the two laborers to repeat the occurrence in his presence.   Rabbi Abraham hereupon informed the Patriarch that they had discovered the sepulchres of the House of David, and of the
kings of Judah.   The Patriarch ordered the place to be
walled up so as to hide it effectually from every one, to
the present day."

That is one version of the story, and here is another:

"The so-called Tomb of David was originally a convent
of Franciscan monks, who believed it to be the site of
the Cœnaculum, and their tradition mentions nothing
of an underground cavern, such as is now said by the
Mohammedans to exist.   The tradition which makes it
the Tomb of David is purely Moslem in its origin, and
does not date back earlier than the time of El Melik ed
Dha'her Chakmak, 1448.   Oral tradition in Jerusalem says
that a beggar came one day to the door of the monastery
asking for relief, and, in revenge for being refused, went
about declaring it was the Tomb of David, in order to
excite the Moslem fanatics to seize upon and confiscate
the spot."

In 1839 Sir Moses Montefiore was permitted to visit
the mosque, and Miss Barclay, the daughter of the celebrated American missionary, at a much more recent date,
was allowed to sketch the tomb.   She says, "The tomb is

apparently an immense sarcophagus of rough stone, and is covered by green satin tapestry, richly embroidered with gold. A satin canopy of red, blue, green and yellow stripes hangs over the tomb, and another piece of black velvet tapestry, embroidered in silver, covers a door in one end of the room, which they said *leads to a cave underneath.* Two small silver candlesticks stand before this door, and a little lamp hangs in the window near it, which is kept constantly burning."

Adjoining the Tomb is the **Cœnaculum, or Chamber of the Last Supper.** It is a plain room, divided into two parts by two columns in the middle, and with pointed vaulting in the ceiling. The place where the table stood, and where our Lord sat, is pointed out to the visitor. The room is 50 feet by 30 feet. In one part is a screen where Mass is celebrated by Christians; in another is a praying place for Moslems. On the wall which separates the Cœnaculum from the Tomb of David many prayers have been written in many languages, the burden being, "Shalum," or Rachel, or Mahmoud, "begs the prayers of David for his (or her) soul."

It is stated that when Titus destroyed Jerusalem, this building, with a few others near it, escaped, and that the earliest travelers to the land found it identified as the scene of the Last Supper. "If it really is the place where our Saviour met with His disciples, it is indeed a holy place, and, on the bare supposition, it cannot be contemplated without a feeling of reverential awe. Nor can we wonder that the Christians in the city flock here on Maundy Thursday to see the Franciscans wash the feet of pilgrims in memory of Him, who in that place taught His disciples, how, in love, they should serve one another."

"And He sendeth forth two of His disciples and saith unto them, Go ye into the city, and there shall meet you

CŒNACULUM (CHAMBER OF THE LAST SUPPER)

a man bearing a pitcher of water; follow him. And wheresoever he shall go in, say ye to the goodman of the house, The Master saith, Where is the guestchamber, where I shall eat the passover with My disciples? And he will shew you a large upper room furnished and prepared : there make ready for us" (Mark 14.13-16).

It is supposed that in this room the disciples were gathered when the Holy Ghost came upon them, and the significance of St. Peter's reference to the adjacent Tomb of David will be readily seen. "Men and brethren, let me freely speak unto you of the patriarch David, that he is both dead and buried, and his sepulchre is with us unto this day" (Acts 2.29).

Re-entering the city by the Zion Gate we pass close to the south wall, where formerly were the wretched huts forming the **Lepers' Quarter.** A more awful spectacle than is presented by these poor creatures cannot be conceived ; they are cut off from association with the outside world, they are literally falling to pieces with disease, limb after limb becoming shapeless, or altogether lost. Some of the faces of these poor creatures are knotted so as to resemble bunches of grapes ; in some the features are scarcely discernible. The disease generally attacks the throat, and causes them to make the peculiar sound which has such a heartrending sadness. It is only within the past two years that this quarter has been demolished. Doubts are entertained whether the present form of leprosy is at all like the disease so often referred to in Scripture. The Leper Hospital was established in 1867. For an account of the law relating to Lepers, see Levit. 13.

From a **watch tower** a short distance from the Lepers' Quarter, there is a celebrated **view** which gives the traveler a better idea of the former positions of buildings, public places and general outlines than from any other spot. He will see the whole of the Mount of Olives, the

valley of Jehoshaphat, and the Kidron, separating Olivet
from the city; the valleys of Gihon and Hinnom running
into the Kidron, north of En-Rogal. South of Hinnom
the Hill of Evil Counsel, with a modern house on the top,
and a tree just beyond, on which it is said that Judas
hanged himself, and, immediately below, the Tyropæon,
or Cheesemongers' Valley, the subject of acres of paper
and rivers of ink (see below).

Following the course of the south wall, and descending
towards the Cheesemongers' Valley, we reach a small
gate in the south wall, called the Dung Gate (Neh. 3.15).
A pathway leads from here to Siloam; the modern name
of the gate is *Bâb-el-Mughâribeh*, or Gate of the Western
Africans. Passing through a jungle of cactus we reach
the southwest wall of the Haram, where I saw some of
the colossal blocks of stone used in the building of that
wonderful structure. In the corner is a stone seventy-
five feet above the foundation, thirty-eight feet four
inches long, and three and a half feet high, and seven feet
wide. Captain Warren sunk a shaft at this corner, to
the foundation of the wall. A few steps north, and we
saw the celebrated spring of the arch which connected
the Temple with the city of Zion. It is called **Robinson's
Arch,** after the name of the great American traveler who
discovered and described it, and rendered immense service in the elucidation of Scripture by his Biblical re-
searches.

The fragments consist of immense stones projecting
from the wall near what is now the level of the ground,
and it forms the spring of what he considered to be a
spacious arch. The wall extends in an unbroken line
from the Wailing Place to the arch, though it cannot be
followed because of the houses which are built up against
it; and, respecting the arch, it is curious to notice that
the second course of the spring contains two stones,

which seem to be two halves, split asunder, of one original stone of enormous dimensions. Whether Robinson's
conclusion was correct remained a disputed point, which
the result of the Exploration has decided in his favor.
Captain Warren sunk several shafts in a line west of this
projecting masonry, and came upon a pier which supported what must have been the west side of the arch.
Beyond all question, at one period there must have been
a bridge here, connecting the Temple with the southwest
part of the city and spanning the valley between. The
excavations also disclosed, at a distance of sixty feet
under the present surface of the soil, fragments of *vous-
soirs*, or beveled stones, lying where they fell, when, by
some means or other unknown, the bridge was destroyed.

By following for a few moments a narrow crooked lane
to the north, and then turning to the right, the **Jews'
Wailing Place** is reached. There is a low wall on the
west side, and on the east the celebrated wall of the
Temple. It is composed of enormous blocks of marble,
each fifteen feet long and three or four feet deep, with
a rough paneled surface, and smooth beveled edge; five
or six courses of this masonry at the bottom bear smaller
stones higher up. Some of the lower stones may have
been at some time disturbed, but many are as they were
first laid. A strange congregation gather here every Friday afternoon, from three until five o'clock, from whence
they go to their synagogues. "It is a strange place to
stand in, the walls towering up so loftily, flowers growing in the crevices, creeping plants swaying to and fro
lazily in the idle wind, and at the foot, are the wailing
Jews. Old men, with black turbans or caps, dressed in
dingy, greasy gabardines, * * * the Hebrew Psalter,
or some other sacred book in hand, the body waving to
and fro, the lips muttering and wailing out lamentation
after lamentation." It is a libel to call this scene a "show

prepared for the benefit of visitors." Jerome makes an affecting allusion to the remnant of mourners in his day who paid the Roman soldiers for allowing them to go and weep over the ruins of the Holy City, and they were no less sincere then than those who weep now over their "holy and beautiful house," defiled by infidels.

"Since the time when the tribe of Abraham went to Jerusalem, the city was called Holy City." "There is something curious about Jews," said a native of Jerusalem. "At the time when Jesus gave the parable of the talents, etc., the political conditions in the Holy Land were then exactly as they are now. The Romans ruled and the Jews occupied the land, hating their rulers. Now the Arabs own the land and they hate their rulers, the Turks. Palestine was then a Roman-conquered province; now it is a Turkish province, occupied by Arabs, the descendants of Abraham.

"People say nowadays that God hasn't kept His promise of giving the land to the Jews as an inheritance forever. He made no such promise; He promised it to Abraham and his seed long before there were any Jews, and so that seed has occupied it ever since.

"There are the descendants of Ishmael and of the ten princes born to him, a multitude that no man can number, who have remained in the country, the property descending from father to son through all generations, so that there are Arabs dwelling on the old inheritance, who can trace their genealogy in a true line back to pre-Israelite days. The Jews have been dispersed, according to prophecy, and now there is no country in the wide world where they cannot be found.

"These Arabs, as well as the Jews, differ in attainments —physical, material and spiritual. Christ was crucified because He was teaching the people to become priests

unto themselves, which was against the government of
Rome and the Temple.

"It is the same to-day—accusations are made that the
Arabs are rising against the government, and their last
appeal is to the Sultan, or as they term him, the supreme
ruler in 'that far country.' "

Describing the conditions of travel to be the same as in
the time of Christ (so far as accommodations for the
native peasants are concerned): "When the Lord of the
vineyard, described in parable, went on his journey to
a far country, he called his servants, gave them certain
trusts and told them to 'occupy' till he returned: That
is they were to represent him in the management of his
property: to do as he would do." That is what Christ
commanded when He went away.   But are Christians
doing it?

The Via Dolorosa

The Via Dolorosa of pilgrims, called by the residents
"The Street of the Palace," leads from the Serai, or
Palace near St. Stephen's Gate, to the Church of the Holy
Sepulchre. It is a narrow street, roughly paved, but in
some places is remarkably picturesque, with arches and
pleasant studies of ancient houses and very old mason-
work. No one can traverse its curious zig-zags and look
at its "holy places" with indifference, as it is sacred
with the tears of many generations of pilgrims, who,
according to their faith, strove to follow in the footsteps
of the Lord. As a mere hard and dry matter of fact,
however, there is no historical evidence whatever for the

sacred sites; the street was not even known until the fourteenth century.

Starting from the Serai, or residence of the Pasha, we will visit the *Stations of the Cross.*

(1) Pilate's **Judgment Hall.**—**The holy steps** (Scala Santa) that led to the Hall, and were trodden by the feet of Christ, were removed to Rome, where I saw them in the Church of St. John Lateran. The spot from whence they were taken is, however, pointed out. The Turkish barracks are now here, and they stand on the site of the ancient Castle of Antonia. At the foot of the steps is: (2) The place of the **Binding of the Cross** upon the shoulder of Christ. Close by here is a Roman Catholic School, "The Sisters of Zion." A few steps further on, where a modern arch spans the street, we enter, on the right, the Church of the Sisters of Zion—first by an iron gate, and then by a wooden door. By turning to the right, I saw, behind a very neat little altar, a part of the **Ecce Homo Arch.** Here we undoubtedly see some of the natural rock; and it has been ascertained that vast rocky vaults are below. The arch is said to have been connected with the Judgment Hall. "Then came Jesus forth, wearing the crown of thorns and the purple robe. And Pilate saith unto them, Behold the man" (John 19.5). Descending now into a street running north and south and turning to the left, is: (3) The place where Christ sunk under the cross. Pilgrims are not agreed as to this Station. The columns in the corner are said by some to mark the spot where they compelled one Simon, a Cyrenian, to carry the cross (Mark 15.21). Turning south to where another street joins, we bend sharply to the right, and in the corner of the wall, to the left, see an indented stone, marking: (4) The **Impression of Christ's Shoulder,** as He leaned there for support. A few steps west, on the left, is: (5) The **House of St,**

Veronica, who wiped the brow of our Saviour, and His features became imprinted upon her handkerchief. On the left is the **Russian Hospital,** said to be over: (7) The spot where Jesus said, "Daughters of Jerusalem, weep not for Me, but for yourselves and your children" (Luke 23.28). From here we follow up the street to where a minaret stands on the left, and by turning into a narrow lane on the right, a few steps bring us to one of the stones that would have cried out if the people had held their peace! A few paces west of the minaret a street comes in on the left, which we follow to where it is spanned by an arch. Here, in the wall to the left, was the old entrance to the Church of the Holy Sepulchre. Here ends the Via Dolorosa. The remainder of the street is a Christian Street; the remainder of the Stations are within the Church of the Holy Sepulchre.

There are two Stations omitted in the foregoing list— the spot where Jesus is said to have met His mother, and the spot where He leaned a second time and left the impression of His hand. Also in the Via Dolorosa may be seen the House of Lazarus, the poor man of the parable, and the. House of Dives, the rich man.

The Abyssinian Monastery

is close to the Church of the Holy Sepulchre; from the Dome in the Court we saw into the Chapel of St. Helena. Here is an olive tree, which the monks point out as marking the spot where Abraham found "the ram caught in the thicket," and was offered in sacrifice in lieu of Isaac. The Abyssinians are a devout body of Christians, passionately attached to the Sacred City, and they seem to know of no higher felicity than to live and die where their Lord lived and died.

[The **Corn Market** is in David Street, and it is said they give Scripture measure; and truly, I saw how they shake the measure, press it down, and cause it to run over. "Give, and it shall be given unto you, good measure pressed down, and shaken together, and running over" (Luke 6.38).]

The Church of St. Anne

is one of the "Holy Places" of Jerusalem. It is situated at the eastern end of the Via Dolorosa, near to St. Stephen's Gate. It was founded in the seventh century, was rebuilt in the twelfth century, converted by Saladin into a school, and in 1856 was presented by the Sultan to the Emperor of the French (Napoleon III.) at the close of the Crimean War. It is said to mark the dwelling-place of St. Anne, the mother of the Virgin; to have been the birth-place of the Holy Mother; the burial-place of her father, Joachim, etc., etc.

"St. Anne left a big sum of money as a fund to this beautiful little church," said a native of Jerusalem, "which was to be used only to cover the expenses of the church."

Round the court of this church are many pepper trees.

Valley of Hinnom

"There is something in the scenery of this valley and
the hill above it; its tombs hewn in the rock, long since
tenantless; the gray gloom of its old fig and olive trees
starting from the fissures of the crags; the overhanging
wall of Zion, desolate almost as in the time of her captivity, that forcibly recall the wild and mournful grandeur of the prophetic writings. Within it, too, is the traditionary **Aceldama**, or **Field of Blood** of the traitor
Judas; a small plot of ground, overhung with one preci-
pice and looking down another into the glen below, on
which is a deep charnel-house, into which it was formerly
the custom to throw the bodies of the dead, as the earth
was supposed to have the power of rapidly consuming
them. The place was selected as the burial place of pilgrims who died at Jerusalem in the Middle Ages. Such
are the scenes that have passed in Hinnom; it is like the
scroll of the prophet, 'written within and without with
mourning, lamentation and woe'" (Bartlett's Walks
about Jerusalem).

Ackeldame is on the southern face of the valley at the
eastern end. There is, however, no historical proof of
this being identical with the "Potters' Field," and it is
known that various sites have, at different times, been
pointed out as the spot where Judas met his death. When
the traitor took back the thirty pieces of silver and "cast
them down in the Temple, and went and hanged himself,

the chief priests took the silver and said, It is not lawful for to put them into the treasury, because it is the price of blood. And they took counsel, and bought with them the Potters' Field, to bury strangers in, wherefore that field was called The Field of Blood unto this day" (Matt. 27.3-10; Acts 1.18,19).

There are many tombs all round about, some of them of hermits, who dwelt here in very early times; some of Crusaders, and some are of recent date. Many of the tombs have beautifully decorated entrances, and some bear inscriptions. There is one tomb called **The Apostles' Cavern,** from a legend that when the disciples "all forsook Him and fled," they came and hid themselves here.

This hill is also called the **Hill of Evil Counsel,** from a tradition that in the country house of Caiaphas, the high priest met the Jews and they took counsel how they might put Him to death. The tradition only dates from the fourteenth century.

Tomb of Absalom and Tombs of the Prophets

Up the valley north of Silwân, on the right, is the **Jews' Cemetery.** The ground is covered with tombstones from the Kidron, half way up the Mount of Olives. On the right of the path are three well-known buildings in the Valley of Jehoshaphat, erected in the Græco-Roman style, popularly called the **Tombs of Zechariah, St. James and Absalom.** That of Zechariah is a square structure of stone, with four pilasters on each side, and a roof of pyramidal shape. "To call this building," as Fergusson justly remarks, "a tomb, is evidently a misnomer, as it is absolutely solid, hewn out of the living rock by cutting

a passage round it. It has no internal chambers, nor
even the semblance of a doorway." The tomb of St.
James is composed of a veranda or screen, cut out of the
rock with two Doric columns, supporting the entablature; at the back of which are extensive excavations containing loculi. The tomb of Absalom is an elaborate
building, square, with columns, in partial relief, standing
out against the wall. There is a smaller square of
masonry above the Ionic cornice, and over that is a circular block, with a singular round tapering roof. The
inside, I saw, is now blocked up with stones, thrown in
according to Arab fashion of execrating the memory of
David's ungrateful son; and by the same means a se-
pulchral cavern behind, styled the tomb of Jehoshaphat,
is hidden from view. The date of these structures is
unknown. No one can reasonably suppose that the tomb
which bears his name is identical with the pillar of Absalom's grave, in the King's Dale. Still, it is not impossible that it may stand on or near the site of that memorial; for by the King's Dale probably is meant the valley
in which this remarkable structure is placed.

The Mount of Olives

Up the Mount of Olives, and near the top, we turn to
the right a few steps, and visit the **Tombs of the
Prophets.** They are on the western part of the Mount of
Olives, and constitute catacombs, winding in a semi-
circular form, with numerous loculi on the sides. Probably the catacombs here were at first natural, and were
then extended and adapted by art; and, like some of the

catacombs at Rome, they have been left in an unfinished
state.

Continuing our walk **as far as Bethany,** we will find
the following extract from Stanley to give a vivid description of the sacred scenes around us, and take us back
to the days of yore:

"In the morning He set forth on His journey. **Three
Pathways** lead, and very probably always led, from
Bethany to Jerusalem; one, a long circuit over the northern shoulder on Mount Olivet, down the valley which
parts it from Scopus; another, a steep footpath over the
summit; the third, the natural continuation of the road
by which mounted travelers always approach the city
from Jericho, over the southern shoulder, between the
summit which contains the Tombs of the Prophets and
that called the Mount of Offence. There can be no doubt
that this last is the road of the Entry of Christ, not only
because, as just stated, it is, and must always have been,
the usual approach for horsemen and for large caravans,
such as then were concerned, but also because this is
the only one of the three approaches which meets the
requirements of the narrative which follows. Two vast
streams of people met on that day. The one poured out
from the city, and as they came through the gardens
whose clusters of palm rose on the southern corner of
Olivet, they cut down the long branches, as was their
wont at the Feast of Tabernacles, and moved upwards
towards Bethany, with loud shouts of welcome. From
Bethany streamed forth the crowds who had assembled
there on the previous night, and who came testifying to
the great event at the sepulchre of Lazarus. The road
soon loses sight of Bethany. It was formerly a rough
mountain track, but is now a broad, well-made carriage
drive; a steep declivity below on the left; the sloping
shoulder of Olivet above on the right; fig trees below

and above, here and there growing out of the rocky soil. Along the road the multitudes threw down the branches cut off from the olive trees through which they were forcing their way, or spread out a rude matting, formed of the palm branches which they had already cut as they came out. The larger portion—those perhaps who had escorted Him from Bethany—unwrapped their loose cloaks from their shoulders, and stretched them along the rough path, to form a momentary carpet as He approached.

"The two streams met mid-way. Half of the vast mass, turning round, preceded; the other half followed. Gradually the long procession swept up and over the ridge, where first begins 'the descent of the Mount of Olives,' towards Jerusalem. At this point the first **View** is caught of the southeastern corner of the city. The Temple, and the more northern portions, are hidden by the slope of Olivet on the right, what is seen is only Mount Zion, now for the most part a rough field, crowned with the Mosque of David and the angle of the western walls, but then covered with houses to its base, surmounted by the Castle of Herod, on the supposed site of the palace of David, from which that portion of Jerusalem, emphatically 'The City of David,' derived its name. It was at this precise point, 'as He drew near, at the descent of the Mount of Olives'—may it not have been from the sight thus opening upon them?—that the hymn of triumph, the earliest hymn of Christian devotion, burst forth from the multitude, 'Hosanna to the Son of *David;* blessed is He that cometh in the name of the Lord. Blessed is the kingdom that cometh of our father David. Hosanna * * * peace * * * Glory in the highest!' There was a pause as the shout rang through the long defile; and as the Pharisees who stood by in the crowd complained, He pointed to the 'stones' which, strewn beneath their feet, would immediately 'cry out if these were to hold their peace.'

"Again the procession advanced. The road descends a slight declivity, and the glimpse of the city is again withdrawn behind the intervening ridge of Olivet. A few moments, and the path mounts again; it climbs a rugged ascent, it reaches a ledge of smooth rock, and in an instant the whole city bursts into view. As now the dome of the Mosque El-Aksa rises like a ghost from the earth before the traveler, so then must have risen the Temple tower; as now the vast enclosure of the Mussulman sanctuary, so then must have spread the Temple-courts; as now the gray town on its broken hills, so then the magnificent city, with its background—long since vanished away—of gardens and suburbs on the western plateau behind.

"Immediately below was the Valley of the Kidron, here seen in its greatest depth as it joins the Valley of Hinnom, and thus giving full effect to the great peculiarity of Jerusalem seen only on its eastern side—its situation as of a city rising out of a deep abyss. It is hardly possible to doubt that this rise and turn of the road, this rocky ledge, was the exact point where the multitude paused again, and He, 'when He beheld the city, wept over it.'

"Nowhere else on the Mount of Olives is there a view like this. By the two other approaches above mentioned, over the summit and over the northern shoulder of the hill, the city reveals itself gradually; there is no partial glimpse, like that which has been just described, as agreeing so well with the first outbreak of popular acclamation; still less is there any point where, as here, the city and Temple would suddenly burst into view, producing the sudden and affecting impression described in the Gospel narrative. And this precise coincidence is the more remarkable, because the traditional route of the

Triumphal Entry is over the summit of Olivet, and the traditional spot of the lamentation is at a place half way down the mountain, to which the description is wholly inapplicable, whilst no tradition attaches to this, the only road by which a large procession could have come, and this, almost the only spot of the Mount of Olives which the Gospel narrative fixes with exact certainty, is almost the only unmarked spot—undefiled or unhallowed by mosque or church, chapel or tower—left to speak for itself, that here the Lord stayed His onward march, and here His eyes beheld what is still the most impressive view which the neighborhood of Jerusalem furnishes, and the tears rushed forth at the sight"—Stanley.

A short distance north of the Tombs of the Prophets, on the **Center Summit of the Mount of Olives,** is a small modern village. "The top of the Mount is not level, but it is notched with three summits, the middle one of which is the highest, on which stands the **Chapel of Ascension.**" The large building, belonging to the Mohammedans, stands on a site which, from the earliest date, has been shown as the place from whence **Our Lord ascended to heaven.** There is a large courtyard, and in the center a small octagonal chapel, with a footprint of Christ. There is a remarkable echo in this chapel, and a hymn sung softly with the proper harmonies, produces an extraordinarily beautiful effect. The great interest, however, of the place is the **view from the Minaret** which ought to be seen again and again.

Very briefly the chief items of the view may be thus summed up: The Holy City lies like a map before us. In the southeast quarter is the Mosque of Omar, standing in the center of the raised platform, or Haram, where Solomon's Temple once stood. To the south of it is El-Aksa, once a Christian church built by Justinian. At the northwest corner of the Temple are the Turkish barracks,

where the Castle of Antonia stood. North of the Temple,
or the southeastern quarter of the city, is the hill Bezetha; and on it, near St. Stephen's Gate, the Church of
St. Anne. West of Bezetha is the hill of Akra, which
is the northwest quarter of the city, and on its eastern
slope stands the Church of the Holy Sepulchre; a little
to the southeast of it are the ruins of the Hospital of the
Knights of St. John. The hill west of Mount Moriah, or
the southwest quarter of the city, is Mount Zion; the
Tower of David, or Hippicus, stands near the Jaffa Gate,
and over it waves the Turkish flag. Southeast of the
tower is the English church, and south of that the Armenian Convent, with a white dome. East of the
convent is the Jewish Quarter, with the two synagogues, one with a green and one with a white dome.
On the top of Zion, south of the wall, is a cluster of buildings; in the midst the black dome marks the Tomb of
David. Turning eastward we see the mountains of Moab
and Gilead, and the Jordan Valley, the course of the
river marked by the dark line of vegetation. South, we
see in the distance, the round topped Frank Mountain;
nearer, almost below, the Hill of Evil Counsel; to the
west of that the Valley of Rephaim. Near the northwest
corner of Jerusalem are the Russian buildings, and beyond Neby Samwil (Mizpeh).

Neby Samwil, or Mizpeh, of the Old Testament, was
a city in Benjamin (Joshua 18.26), and here the great
national assemblies of Israel were held in the time of
the Judges. "Then all the children of Israel went out,
and the congregation was gathered together as one man,
from Dan even to Beersheba, with the land of Gilead,
unto the Lord in Mizpeh" (Judges 20.1).

When Samuel mourned over the sins of Israel, he said,
"Gather all Israel to Mizpeh, and I will pray for you
unto the Lord. And they gathered together to Mizpeh"

(1 Sam. 12.5,6). One of the most remarkable scenes in Mizpeh was when a young man was brought hither, and "when he stood among the people he was higher than any of the people from his shoulders and upwards * * * and all the people shouted and said, God save the king" (1 Sam. 10.24,25), and Saul became their king. It was between Mizpeh and Shen that "Samuel took a stone * * * and called the name of it Ebenezer, saying Hitherto the Lord hath helped us" (1 Sam. 7.6-12). The town was fortified by Asa (1 Kings 15.22). Gedaliah was assassinated here (2 Kings 25.23-25); and when, in the time of Nehemiah, the wall of Jerusalem was rebuilt, the men of Mizpeh joined with the men of Gibeon in rebuilding one portion of the wall (Neh. 3.7, 15, 19).

Continuing on the Mount of Olives, the view from the Minaret above mentioned, the northern ridge of Olivet is Scopus, beyond which is a small village among olive trees named Shafat.   To the right of it is a hill, the ancient Nob, and two miles beyond, Gibeah, the home of Saul; three miles further north is Ramah, the birthplace of Samuel, and three miles beyond that Bireh, the ancient Beeroth—one of the four Hivite or Gibeonite cities that made the league with Joshua (Joshua 9.17).   Such is a brief catalogue of the view, the most wonderful and interesting in all the world.

The summit of Olivet is about two hundred feet above the city of Jerusalem; and on the south of the summit is a Roman Catholic church, **"The Church of Pater Noster,"** the traditional spot where our Lord taught His disciples the **"Lord's Prayer."** A French princess (the Princess Latour d'Auvergne) has caused a curious new building to be erected here.   In the court are thirty-six panels, with the Lord's Prayer written in thirty-six different languages, so that pilgrims from all parts of the world can read the prayer in their own language.

Near the foot of the mountain lies the Garden of
Gethsemane. Beyond and about four hundred feet below
us the little Brook Kidron trickled through the narrow
Valley of Jehoshaphat.

In order to continue the **Tour** of the places of interest
outside the Walls of Jerusalem, we descend, from the
Mount of Olives by the northern road, the way which
David ascended when he fled from Absalom. "And
David went up by the ascent of Mount Olivet, and wept
as he went, and had his head covered, and he went bare-
foot" (2 Sam. 15.30).

On the western slope of Olivet, near the Brook Kidron, is the

Garden of Gethsemane

The space enclosed is about one-third of an acre, and
is surrounded by a wall covered with some kind of a
plaster. The wall is about eleven feet high. Within the
enclosure the garden is surrounded by an iron fence.
Between the stone wall and the iron railing is a wide
path. The tradition which places it here is of considerable antiquity. Eusebius, Bishop of Cæsarea, speaks of
the garden as well known; Jerome repeats the same testimony. It is entered by a gate kept under lock and key,
under the control of the Franciscans. Within the garden
are **eight olive trees** which are undoubtedly of great age,
and may have sprung from the roots of those which were
here in the time of our Lord, and may even be the original trees. These trees are about thirty-five feet in circumference. Small, sanctified pictures, fourteen in all,
representing the fourteen traditionary stations of Christ,

GARDEN OF GETHSEMANE—ONE OF THE ANCIENT OLIVE TREES,
UNDER WHICH JESUS PRAYED.

are painted on the walls. The Franciscan monks point out the **Chapel of the Agony,** in a cave; the rocky place where the disciples slept; the spot where Judas gave the kiss of betrayal.

In the middle of the Garden a wealthy American lady is buried. Over her tomb is the inscription: "Adeline Whelan from Washington, was buried here in 1875." "That was the lady who built the well in the center of this garden," explained the monk, "and the fountain supplies water for moistening the ground and cultivating a few flowers." This Garden is the property of the Catholics. As we were leaving the old Franciscan brother handed to me a bouquet of flowers and our conductor presented us with some leaves from the ancient olive trees, which he had received from the old Franciscan monk. "Jesus went over the Brook Kidron with His disciples, where there was a garden into which He entered" (Matt. 26.36; Mark 14.32).

A writer, who looks upon this as the veritable scene of the agony and betrayal, an opinion which is shared by many eminent travelers and writers, says: "Over there in Jerusalem His body was crucified; but here was the scene of the crucifixion of His soul. *There* the letter of the law was executed, but here the awful weight of its spirit was borne. There he drank the dregs of sorrow, but here the 'full cup' was wrung out of Him. Here the enemy who had departed from Him for a season, returned with all the powers of hell to overthrow the Son of Man. Here his 'own familiar friend' betrayed Him. Here the Captain of our Salvation was made perfect through suffering, and from this place, broken hearted as He was, with the Cross before Him, and a heavier cross upon Him, He rose up from the garden and went forth to die. 'Take off thy shoes from off thy feet, for the place whereon thou standest is holy ground.'"

"On over Olivet is a steep path up and down which late in the evening or early in the morning Jesus walked to and from His ministry in Jerusalem. For it is not written that Jesus ever spent a night in that city, until that night when He was dragged up there before the judgment-seat. When the evening came and the disciples went to their own homes, Jesus went out to the Mount of Olives to spend the night in prayer, or to the quiet village of Bethany (page 131), where awaited Him restful welcome from the three friends He loved. In Bethany was a home honored above all others by the frequent visits of the Son of God, a home where our Saviour and His disciples found welcome and rest and entertainment. In Bethany the sisters spread a thanksgiving feast to Him who raised their brother from the dead, and brought out the very valuable ointment" (page 132).

A short distance from Gethsemane, in the bed of Kidron, north of the road, is the

Tomb of the Virgin

A handsome flight of forty-seven steps leads to the church, which according to some traditions was erected by St. Helena. The whole place, which belongs now to the Greeks, is full of legends, and many sacred spots once here have been transferred elsewhere, and *vice versa*. Here are the tombs of Joachim and Anna, the parents of the Virgin (page 78), the Tomb of Joseph, the husband of the Virgin, the Tomb of Mary, and the Grotto of the Agony (page 89). Here, too, are praying places, or altars, for Greeks, Armenians, Abyssinians and Moslems. The guide said that the small chapel at the end of

the Grotto contained the empty tomb of the Virgin. Near
this tomb are twenty-six oil lamps of pure silver, and six
candles burn over the top of it. It is of marble, and from
the center rises a little chimney to carry away the smoke
from the lamps and candles. Outside are about a hundred oil lamps, some of which belong to the Greeks and
some to the Armenians. There is a very old clock to
be seen, the pendulum of which is brilliantly set with
jewels. A flight of steps leads down inside the door to
the church.

The Greeks claim that this is the oldest Christian
church in the world. They perform a service here every
morning from 7 to 8.30 a. m., and it is open all day on
Festivals. At other times visitors should knock at the
little iron door on the south side of the church. The
arch and pillars of this entrance date from the twelfth
century. From the Kidron we ascend the hill to St.
Stephen's Gate, passing the traditional spot where St.
Stephen was stoned. Recent explorations tend to prove
that the real site of St. Stephen's death was outside the
Damascus Gate.

The view from St. Stephen's Gate is remarkable.
Across the narrow valley rises the Mount of Olives. The
top is not level, but is notched with three summits, the
middle one of which is the highest, on which stands the
Chapel of the Ascension. Three paths, deeply worn, lead
over the Mount (see page 82). The enclosure of Gethsemane, at the foot of the Mount, is well seen from here
(page 88). On our left, under the wall, is a large reservoir, the Hamman Sitti Mayam, or Bath of Our Lady,
where people come to draw water and to bathe. On the
right is the Mohammedan Cemetery, covering a great
part of the eastern slope of Moriah.

Continuing past the northeast corner of the city walls
and striking off to the north, northwest, a journey of
about half an hour brings us to the

Tombs of the Kings (or Helena)

Three classes of excavated tombs are found in Palestine:

1. Those consisting of deep loculi cut in the face of soft limestone, and closed up by rough stone slabs.

2. Those formed into square or oblong chambers cut in the rock. Deep loculi are ranged along the sides, "their mouths, closed by neatly dressed stone slabs, fitting closely into reveals made to receive them. The entrance to the chamber is by a low square opening, fitted with a slab in the same manner, or with a stone door, turning on a socket hinge, and secured by bolts on the inside. In this kind of tomb there is usually a bench, running in front of the loculi, and elevated from a foot and a half to three feet above the floor of the excavation." There are tombs on Mount Ebal with benches without loculi, the bench being the resting-place for the corpse.

3. Those in which one entrance leads into a number of chambers. The Tombs of the Judges (page 93), the Tombs of the Prophets (page 80), and the Tombs of the Kings are all of this class.

"The Tombs of the Kings are the most interesting of all these remains. They lie to the north of Jerusalem, about half a mile beyond the Damascus Gate. * * * On the left side, at the end of the portico, * * * there is a very low door, which one must stoop to enter, and by it is a large stone, which may be rolled so as to close the opening. It reminded me of a large mill-stone and would certainly require a good deal of strength to move it along the groove cut for its reception. Having entered within the low door, I found myself in a spacious chamber forming a square, whence passages led into other square chambers, round which were numerous deep loculi, with inner and very small chambers beyond them, or at their side. Turning out of the large principal ante-chamber to the west, and passing through a second chamber, I ascended a flight of steps which led to a higher chamber on the north. There lies the broken lid of a sarcophagus (a limestone coffin) and a sarcophagus taken from this chamber is now preserved in the Louvre at Paris. I noticed, connected with the loculi, ledges to support slabs for closing them in, after the dead should be deposited there. * * * The architecture points to the Roman times, and it seems pretty clear that the catacombs bearing the name of the kings, never could have been prepared for the ancient princes of Judah. Not here are we to look for the Tomb of David and his descendants. Mr. Fergusson considers that they belong to the time of Herod"—(Dr. Stoughton).

The opinion is now very generally entertained that this is the Tomb of *Queen Helena of Adiabene,* a convert to Judaism, 48 A. D., and who, according to Josephus, was buried here.

About a quarter of an hour to the northwest are the so-called **Tombs of the Judges,** which have in front an architectural *façade* with an ornamental pediment, and in the angular space beneath is a pedimented doorway. Through this we enter into spacious catacombs, with deep loculi ranged along the sides in three stories; the upper stories with ledges in front to facilitate the introduction of bodies into the narrow cells, and to support the stones which close up the cells. This arrangement may be regarded as characteristically a Jewish one.

We will continue, however, and take this middle road which leads direct to the Damascus Gate.

Near the Damascus Gate is the **Grotto of Jeremiah,** where a tradition, dating from the fourteenth century, says the Prophet wrote the Book of Lamentations, and was subsequently buried. The rocky tombs, cisterns and other excavations are extremely interesting. The place belongs to the Moslems, and the traveler need not hesitate to drive a hard bargain with the custodian (or guardian), who sometimes demands absurdly high fees for admission.

Opposite the Grotto of Jeremiah, and close to the Damascus Gate are the

Subterranean Quarries

The entrance is through a hole, only large enough to creep through. Then a vast succession of mighty aisles and mammoth chambers are reached, where we walked through cavern after cavern, and aisle after aisle, till we seemed to have gone the whole length and breadth of the city. The exploration should not be attempted without a guide, or a reliable compass, and a large ball of twine to be used and fastened as a clue. It is not yet known how far these quarries extend. That they are of very ancient date is certain; and there is great probability that they yielded the stones used in the building of the Temple; for "the house when it was in building was built of stone made ready before it was brought thither, so that there

was neither hammer nor axe, nor any tool of iron heard
in the house while it was building" (1 Kings 6.7).

Many a poetical passage has been written by travelers
who have explored this underground Jerusalem, discovered in 1852 by Dr. Barclay.

The author of "On Holy Ground," says: "There was a
strange feeling of awe in walking through these subterranean caverns, for there in the rock we could make out
the marks of chiselings just as they were left centuries
and centuries ago. There was the hole where once a
spring of water trickled, and at which the weary workmen slaked their thirst; there were the niches for the
lamps of the quarrymen, and there were huge blocks
partially cut from the rocks, and pillars partially shaped
and left unfinished. And for ages and ages the darkness
and silence have dwelt together in these dreary caverns,
while overhead, in the city, generations have come and
gone; its streets have been deluged with blood, and its
glories have been leveled with the dust. And here silence
and darkness dwelt when the cry of 'Crucify Him, crucify Him!' rang through the busy streets above, and a
shudder ran through these gloomy regions when the cry
went forth, 'It is finished!' and a great earthquake shook
the solid earth, while darkness enfolded the land."

From the Damascus Gate, the finest in Jerusalem, we
continued round the walls to the Jaffa Gate, and by this
route made a complete circuit of the city.

North of the Jaffa Gate—the busiest in Jerusalem—on
the road to Jaffa (page 18), are the **Russian Buildings,**
very ugly, but doubtless very useful, including a capital hospital, schools, cathedral, accommodation for a
thousand pilgrims, etc. There is a fine **view** from the
church, and on the west side near the door is an immense
column, perhaps intended for the Temple, and broken
in the endeavor to raise it.

In this neighborhood are two very interesting and deserving philanthropic institutions, the **Talitha-Kumi**
("which is, being interpreted, Damsel, I say unto thee,
arise," Mark 5.41); an orphanage for girls founded by
the deservedly popular Rheinish-Westphalian deaconesses; Schneller's **Orphanage for Boys,** where over seventy boys are well educated and taught some useful
branch of industry.

One of the deaconesses, who several years ago came
from the convent at Kaiserweith, Rheinland (which is
the old Homeland of the writer), took my beloved wife
and me through the building, and I must state that all
the rooms and everything we saw were very clean indeed, and in proper and healthy condition. The orphans
looked very bright and cheerful and the kindness and
courtesy of this deaconess are appreciated by all.

From Jerusalem to Bethlehem

(This is a journey of 1½ hours' riding, or one hour in
a carriage. The road is in very good order.)

Leaving Jerusalem by the Jaffa Gate, we descend into
the Valley of Gihon, and cross it at the upper end of the
lower pool; then ascend the hill on the southwest side
to the "Valley of the Giants," leaving on the left the traditional tree on which Judas hanged himself, and the
country house of Caiaphas the High Priest. This plain
has been called the **Valley of Rephaim**, the boundary-
line between Judah and Benjamin (Joshua 20.8). It was
here that the Philistines were defeated by David. Before
reaching the top of the long rise, we were shown a well,
which is called the **Well of the Magi,** tradition stating
that the *Wise Men*, after leaving the presence of Herod,

knew not whither to go, and being weary with their
journey, stooped to draw water, when they saw the star
reflected in the well, and under its guidance they followed till it stood over where the holy child was. Our
guide pointed out a great rock by the roadside where
Elijah, wearied in his flight from Jezebel, lay down to
rest. It seemed a hard bed for a tired man, but we remembered that in olden times rocks and caves were selected for sleeping-places, and stones often served for
pillows. At this point Jerusalem is visible behind, and
Bethlehem in front.

Descending the hill, in about twenty minutes from
Mar Elyâs, the **Tomb of Rachel** is reached. It is a small
modern building with a dome. There can be no doubt
whatever that this site, which is revered by Christians
and Moslems, as well as by the Jews, is the scene of the
touching story of Rachel's death.

She had journeyed from Bethel to this place, on the
way to Bethlehem. "And there was but a little way to
come to Ephrath" (Bethlehem); not more than a mile,
and within full sight of the spot. Here she was delivered of her son. "And it came to pass, as her soul was
in departing (for she died), that she called his name
Ben-oni (i. e., son of my sorrow.): but his father called
him Benjamin" (i. e., son of my right hand.); "And
Rachel died, and was buried in the way to Ephrath,
which is Bethlehem. And Jacob set a pillar upon her
grave: that is the pillar of Rachel's grave unto this day"
(Genesis 35.16-20). The reader will remember that in
wooing her, seven long years "seemed to Jacob but a few
days, for the love he bore her." And as the old man,
long weary years after her death, was himself drawing
to the grave, he repeats, with tender memory the story
of his loss. "And as for me, when I came from Padan,
Rachel died by me in the land of Canaan in the way,

when yet there was but a little way to come unto Ephrath; and I buried her there in the way of Ephrath; the
same is Bethlehem" (Genesis 48.7).

About a quarter of a mile to the west of Rachel's Tomb
is a village named **Beit Jâla**, the residence of the Latin
and Greek Patriarchs. It has a population of 3,000,
mostly Greeks, and all Christians. It is possible that this
village may be the ancient *Zelyah,* where Saul was met
by the messengers of Samuel, saying, "The asses which
thou went to seek are found, and lo thy father hath left
the care of the asses, and sorroweth for thee, saying,
What shall I do for my son" (1 Sam. 9.10).

The views of Bethlehem, as the ancient city is approached, are extremely picturesque, and will doubtless
suggest many pictures to the mind's eye in connection
with the stories of Ruth, David, and others. Here is a
specimen of the pictures:—

"There are so many events connected with Bethlehem
that it is hard to single out cases; but one cannot look
upon that group of women in their white robes, standing
over there on a terrace just under the town (as it appears from our view, gesticulating to one another in
earnest conversation), without thinking of the group
that once surrounded Naomi, the sorrow-stricken widow,
returning to her native town, and hearing the people
say, as they looked at her pale, haggard face, 'Is this
Naomi?'

"Nor can we look upon the corn-fields, with their green
blades waving on the morning air, without thinking of
the time of harvest, when Ruth gleaned in the field after
the reapers, and Boaz saw her and loved her for her
love, so that by and by she became his wife, and when a
child was born to her in process of time, she became the
grandmother of David the King, and the ancestress of
Christ. It is a charming story, and I know not that I

ever read a romance with a tithe of the interest that
I read the story of Ruth that morning on the way to
Bethlehem.

"But see! over there, coming down the steep pathway on one side of the town, is a shepherd leading forth
his sheep. He goeth before them, and the sheep follow
him. He is leading them out to green pastures; they
know him, and follow whithersoever he leadeth; the fore-
most of them are not more than a foot behind the shepherd's heels. It was upon one of these hills that David,
the youth, 'ruddy, and withal of a beautiful countenance,
and goodly to look to,' kept his father's sheep. It was
in these glens and valleys that he rang out those glorious
songs which have echoed through the world, and been
the key-notes to new melodies in every believer's heart.
It was here that the rocks and the hills, the sun-
shine and the shadow, the poetry and the music of the
little world around him, became God's instruments to
create that mighty world within him whose treasures
have enriched all ages. It was from those terraces yonder that he would see the starry heavens, declaring the
glory of God, and cry out in humility and faith, 'What
is man that Thou art mindful of him?' Truly, Bethlehem is still the 'City of David' (Luke 2.4); and every
hill, and valley, and field recalls some story of his life.
Now we see him coming from that wild glen, bearing
the trophies of his battles with the lion and the bear;
or we see him hurrying, with eager heart and wondering
countenance, to meet the prophet who had sent for him
from the fields, and who anointed him in the midst of
his brethren. Again, we watch him coming down that
steep hill with the ass laden by his father, on his way
to Saul, and we note the tender care with which he holds
the harp, that friend of his solitude and minister of his

joy—that instrument which shall be in his hand as powerful over the giant Saul as the sling and the stone (his boyhood's toys) shall be over the giant Goliath."

Bethlehem (Beit-Lahm)

Bethlehem (House of Bread), or Beit-Lahm, is situated six miles from Jerusalem, on an elongated hill, well cultivated in terraces round the sides, and with fertile corn fields in the valley below. On the terraces, vines and fig trees are in abundance. The wine of Bethlehem has considerable local celebrity, but does not appear to be appreciated by some travelers.

The town consists of about five hundred houses, mostly substantial, and the fortress-like buildings of the Church of the Nativity and the three adjoining convents. The streets are narrow, steep, and slippery. Bethlehem forms a pleasing picture, the square solid-built houses, with a good sprinkling of cupolas rising above each other like the gardens and groves just below them.

The population is about 8,000. The inhabitants of Bethlehem have always been celebrated for their ruddy beauty, and also for their fierce turbulence, inclined, like David, to be "men of war from their youth," and, it is said, always conspicuous in the frequent religious disturbances at Jerusalem. Bethlehem is the most Christian town in Palestine; the Moslem Quarter was destroyed by Ibrahim Pasha after a rebellion in 1834.

The inhabitants are largely employed in the manufacture and sale of bracelets, beads, rosaries, crucifixes, cigar-holders, and various other small articles, chiefly made of olive and Dead Sea wood and mother-of-pearl.

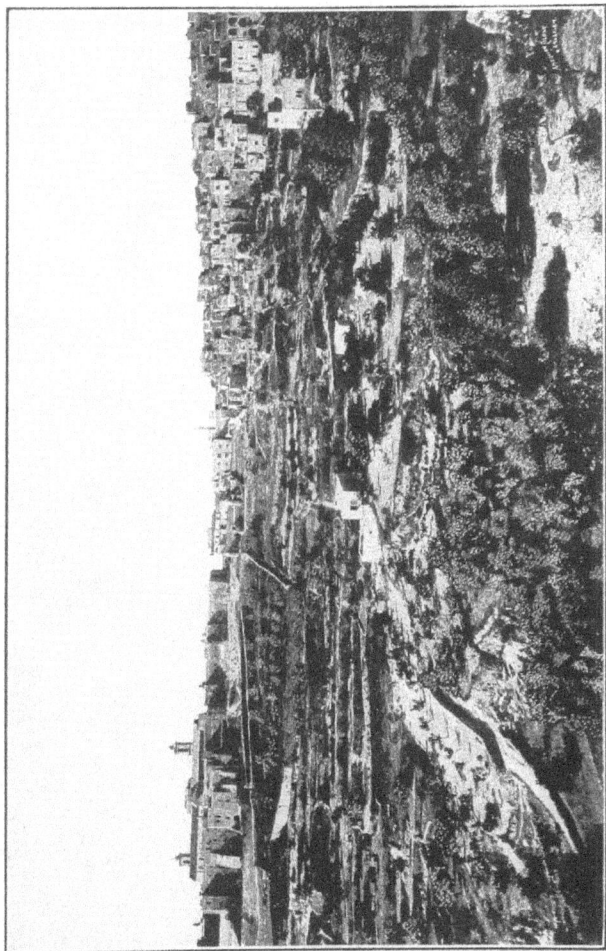

BETHLEHEM.

Bible Associations

An event of importance in connection with Bethlehem is the anointing of David by Samuel to be King of Israel (1 Sam. 16.13). In the adjacent hill country, the shepherd boy, the great-grandson of Ruth, had spent his youth in tending sheep; there he had encountered wild beasts (1 Sam. 17.37), and composed his earliest Psalms. From Bethlehem he was sent for by Saul, to "minister to a mind diseased" with his melodious harpings (1 Sam. 16.19). Returning from the courts of Saul to his native place (1 Sam. 17), he thence goes forth to see his brothers with the army, and slays the giant champion of Philistia, as recorded in the same chapter.

There were other members of the family of Jesse who attained to celebrity, and displayed the fighting character of the Bethlehemite in all their actions. These were Joab, Abishai, and Asahel, the sons of David's sister Zeruiah, and Amasa, the son of David's other sister Abigail (1 Chron. 2.16). When Asahel, "light of foot as a wild roe" (2 Sam. 2.18) outstripped his companions in the pursuit of Abner, and met his death at the hands of that chieftain, the servants of David "buried him in the sepulchre of his father, which was in Bethlehem" (2 Sam. 2.32). Well might the little town take as one of its titles the appellation of "the City of David" (Luke 2.4), for Bethlehem and its neighborhood was the scene of his earliest associations and exploits and spiritual exercises; and the home of his nearest kindred.

From the able arguments of Hepworth Dixon there seems good reason to believe that through all these long years of peace and war, of captivity and restoration, there was a continuity of possession on the part of the family of David, of their ancestral lands on the hill of Bethlehem. And more, there seems no reason to doubt that on the patrimony of Boaz, and Jesse, and Chimham, there had been erected, by one of the heads of the family, in accordance with eastern custom, a caravanserai or inn, representative of the primitive hospitality of earlier days; so that when "Joseph went up from Galilee, out of the city of Nazareth, into Judæa, unto the city of David, which is called Bethlehem (because he was *of the house and lineage of David*), to be taxed with Mary his espoused wife" (Luke 2.4,5), he was, in coming to the inn, not only literally complying with the Roman edict, that every one should go to his own city, but was probably going to his own house.

And now there came to pass the wondrous events recorded in detail by the evangelists Matthew and Luke, in the second chapters of their respective gospels, and succinctly summed up by St. John in the statement that, "The Word was made flesh and dwelt amongst us." It is these events which make Bethlehem a household word wherever Christianity is professed, and cause the thoughts of millions to be turned towards this Judæan village, as year by year Christmas-tide comes round. "And thou, Bethlehem-Ephratah, though thou be little among the thousands of Judah, yet out of thee shall He come forth unto me that is to be ruler in Israel; whose goings forth have been from of old, from everlasting" (Micah 5.2).

It is in commemoration of the great event thus foretold by Micah, years before its occurrence, and the kindred associations linked with that event, that the principal object of attraction in Bethlehem, about to be described, was erected.

The Church of the Nativity

The huge fortress-like pile of buildings at the eastern extremity of the village of Bethlehem comprises the Church of the Nativity, and the three contiguous convents belonging respectively to the Catholic, Greek, and Armenian churches.

The *Nave* of the Church, which is the common property of all Christians, and wears a very desolate and neglected aspect, is the "oldest monument of Christian architecture in the world." It is the sole remaining portion of the grand Basilica erected here by the Empress Helena, the mother of Constantine, in 327 A. D. In this edifice, once brilliant with gold and colored marbles, Baldwin was crowned, and the last repairs were executed by Edward IV. of England.

The Church is still a fine building. It contains five rows of about 40 marble columns, of Corinthian order, each of a single stone (Pressensé), some of which are said to have once formed a part of the Temple at Jerusalem. The mosaics on the walls, considered to date from the original construction of the edifice, are mostly faded, but here and there are in good condition. The roof is formed of beams of rough cedar from Lebanon.

The Chapel or Grotto of the Nativity is a cave in the rock, over and around which the Church and Convent buildings are reared, and for the sake of which they exist. It is twenty feet below the floor of the church, and is approached by two spiral staircases.

Descending by either of these staircases, we enter a vault 33 feet by 11 feet, encased with Italian marble, and decorated with thirty gold and silver lamps, which throw a dim soft light on the place below, and with figures of saints, decorated with embroidery and various other ornaments.

On one side of the Grotto is a recess where a silver star on the pavement indicates the spot where our Saviour was born. Around it is the inscription

"Hic De Virgine Maria Jesus Christus Natus est."
("Here was born Jesus Christ of the Virgin Mary.")

Above this spot sixteen silver lamps are perpetually burning (six belong to the Greeks, and five each to the Catholics and Armenians). Close by, there is a plain altar, which each of the three sects use on their special festivals, and decorate according to their own ideas.

The other recess, the **Chapel of the Manger**, is said to be the place of the discovery of the wooden manger or præsepium (shown now at the church of St. Maria Maggiore at Rome).

The **Altar of the Magi,** the property of the Catholics, is said to mark the spot where the Wise Men of the East presented their gifts.

In proximity to the Grotto of the Nativity, various chapels, tombs, pictures, etc., are shown.

The **Chapel of St. Joseph** is described as the spot to which Joseph retired at the moment of the Nativity, and where the angel appeared, commanding the Flight into Egypt.

The **Altar of the Innocents** is overlooked by a picture of no merit. **Thousands** of victims of Herod's cruel massacre are alleged to be buried here.

Whatever may be thought of some of the above-named altars, it seems extremely probable that the Grotto of the Nativity may indeed be the actual place of our Lord's birth. That a cave, or caves, in the hillside adjacent to the inn, or small hotel, were utilized as stables for the cattle, especially when the inn was crowded, and that in such a cave the Redeemer was born, is a tradition of very high antiquity. It was commonly accepted as early as the time of Justin Martyr, about a hundred years after the facts occurred.

Of one ardent believer in the *Grotto* as his Saviour's birthplace, lasting memorials are seen in the **Chapel and Tomb of St. Jerome.** The chapel is the cell where that illustrious champion of the church spent the greater part of his life. The following eloquent passage, from Dean Stanley's "Sinai and Palestine," graphically describes those long years of vigil and toil:

"If the traveler follows the windings of that long subterranean gallery [as the author has done], he will find himself, at its close, in a rough chamber hewn out of the rock; here sufficiently clear to need no proof of vindication. In this cell, in all probability, lived and died the most illustrious of all the pilgrims attracted to the cave of Bethlehem, the only one, of the many hermits and monks, from the time of Constantine to the present day, sheltered within its rocky sides, whose name has traveled beyond the limits of the Holy Land. Here, for more than thirty years, beside what he believed to be literally the cradle of the Christian faith, Jerome fasted, prayed, dreamed, and studied; here he gathered round him his devoted followers in the small communities which formed the beginnings of conventual life in Pal-

estine; here the fiery spirit which he had brought with
him from his Dalmatian birthplace, and which had been
first roused to the religious fervor on the banks of the
Moselle, vented itself in the flood of treatises, letters, and
commentaries, which he poured forth from his retire-
ment, to terrify, exasperate, and enlighten the Western
World; here also was composed the famous translation
of the Scriptures which is still the 'Biblia Vulgata' (or
Bible version) of the Latin Church; and here took place
that pathetic scene, his last communion and death—at
which all the world has been permitted to be present in
the wonderful picture of Domenichino, which has represented in colors never to be surpassed, the attenuated
frame of the weak and sinking flesh,—the resignation and
devotion of the spirit ready for its immediate departure."

I remember Domenichino's famous painting in the
Vatican at Rome, called "Last Communion of St. Jerome."

Before leaving this wonderful group of buildings, com-
prehended under the general title of "The Church of the
Nativity," and, after ascending the stairs of the Crypt,
we visited the Catholic **Church of St. Catherine,** hand-
somely decorated, and then passed into the **Franciscan
Monastery,** with its very pleasant gardens. From the
roof of the Armenian Monastery is a fine view.

The **Well of Bethlehem,** or David's well, may be visited on the way from Jerusalem, and before entering the
town, or it is an easy and pleasant walk of about fifteen
minutes. It is the traditional spot referred to in 2 Sam.
23.13-17, and 1 Chron. 11.15-19. When David and his
men were in the Cave of Adullam, and Bethlehem was
garrisoned by the Philistines, David expressed the longing desire, "Oh, that one would give me to drink of the
water of the well of Bethlehem, that is at the gate!"
Three mighty men heard the wish, broke through the

SHEPHERDESS.

Philistine hosts, and brought their lord the cooling draught he had longed for. But David would not drink that which his followers had risked their lives to bring him, and poured it out before the Lord.

A short distance south of the Church of the Nativity is the **Milk Grotto**, the traditional scene of the seclusion of the Virgin Mary and the holy infant Jesus before the flight into Egypt. It is alleged that a drop of the Virgin's milk having fallen upon the floor turned the whole cavern white, and that to this day the cavern has the curious property of increasing the milk of women who visit it in their need. Those who cannot visit it are supposed to derive benefit from eating a kind of biscuit in which the dust of the rock is mixed.

A short distance east of the Milk Grotto is the so-called House of Joseph, and beyond this the village of Beit Sâhûr, where the shepherds of Luke 2 are supposed to have resided. In about fifteen minutes, the **Shepherds' Field** is reached. A very ancient tradition makes this the spot where the shepherds were watching their flocks by night, and received "the good tidings of great joy." "And there were in the same country shepherds abiding in the field, keeping watch over their flock by night. And lo! the angel of the Lord came upon them, and the glory of the Lord shone round about them; and they were sore afraid. And the angel said, Fear not; for, behold, I bring you good tidings of great joy, which shall be to all people. For unto you is born this day in the city of David a Saviour, which is Christ the Lord. And this shall be a sign unto you: Ye shall find the babe wrapped in swaddling clothes, laying in a manger. And suddenly there was with the angel a multitude of the heavenly host praising God, and saying, Glory to God in the highest, and on earth peace, good will toward men."

A wall encloses this field, in which there are some fine

olive trees. The **Grotto of the Shepherds** is in the field—
a dark subterranean chapel belonging to the Greeks
When the eye becomes accustomed to the darkness, it
will be found that the Grotto is fitted up as a church,
and contains a few paintings. It is alleged that this is
the identical spot where the shepherds beheld the vision
of the angel—a tradition which has no authority and
dates from the time of the Crusaders.

From Jerusalem to Hebron

(By the Pools of Solomon.)

The road from Jerusalem is the same as that described
in the previous route as far as Beit Jâla (page 98);
here it leaves Bethlehem on the left and branches off to
the right, and the distance to the Pools is about one
hour. The interesting and important excursion by carriage from Jerusalem to Bethlehem, the Pools of Solomon
and Hebron, and back to Jerusalem, can be done in one
day.

We started at 7 a. m. and returned at about 6 p. m.

Pools of Solomon.—There is near the Upper Pool a
huge building, with castellated walls of uncertain origin
—though obviously Saracenic. It has been called a castle, but probably always was, what it now is, a khân (or
inn). A short distance to the right of the castle is the
Sealed Fountain of Solomon (Song Sol. 4.12) which, it
is said, regulated and secured the constant supply of
water for the Holy City. To visit it, candles had to be
taken, as it was approached by a flight of twenty steps
leading into a dark vaulted chamber. In the dry season
this spring supplies the Pools with water.

The **Pools** are three enormous cisterns of marble ma
sonry, and their measurements are:

"Lower Pool. Length, 582 feet; breadth, **east end,**
207 feet, west, 148 feet; depth at east end, 50 feet. (Dr.
Thomson says that 'when full it would float the largest
man-of-war that ever ploughed the ocean.')"

"Middle Pool. Distance above Lower Pool, 248 feet;
length, 423 feet; breadth, at east end, 250 feet; west, 160
feet; depth at east end, 39 feet.

"Upper Pool. Distance above Middle Pool, 160 feet;
length, 380 feet; breadth, east end, 236, west, 229 feet;
depth at west end, 25 feet." (Robinson.)

From the admirable state of preservation these basins
are in, it is difficult to realize that they are more than a
century old; it is most probable, however, that they date
from Solomon's time, although they were restored by
Pontius Pilate. Formerly water was supplied to Jerusalem from these pools; at the present time water is only
conveyed as far as Bethlehem, although the course of
the aqueduct can be traced all the way to the Haram, or
court of the Temple, a distance of twelve to fourteen
miles (page 65).

The name of Solomon's Pools is taken from a passage
in Eccles. 2.6, "I made me *pools of water* to water therewith the wood that bringeth forth trees."

For three hours there is nothing to describe of our
journey; we crossed valleys and spurs of hills, where
traces of terraces were visible and passed merchantmen
with their camel trains. The vegetation attracted our
attention, especially the hills wooded with small oaks,
terebinths, and arbutus.

"At length our course lay over a stony, dangerous road,
a long lane of slippery slabs; and here our thoughts were
diverted from camels, and Arabs, and the trifling things
which even in the Holy Land engage one's thoughts.

We were on the old road to Hebron—perhaps on the oldest road in the world. Along it Abraham passed on that journey of faith to sacrifice his son on Moriah; along it David led his veterans to conquer the stronghold of the Jebusites on Zion; and along it, perhaps, the Saviour was borne in His mother's arms on the way to Egypt. A crowd of thoughts rushed through the mind as we looked around upon the scenes of fertility and desolation. We needed not to have the ruins of convent-walls, or the legends of monks and bookmakers, to impress us with the wonders of the locality. These hills, and roads, and valleys are sacred to the memory of Abraham, the Father of the Faithful and the Friend of God. Here, in the bitterness of his sorrow, after Sarai was 'buried out of his sight' in the Cave of Machpelah, no doubt he wandered, and looking up at the bright stars in the cloudless sky, which had been typical to him aforetime of the power and goodness of God in the days of his prosperity, he looked at again through his tearful eyes, and read in them a pledge still of the goodness and faithfulness of the Almighty. Here Isaac, and Jacob, and David, and Solomon walked, revolving in their minds the destiny of that nation which might have been at this day the center of universal empire; but the scattered tribes are spread through the nations of the world." (Hodder.)

Hebron

Hebron (Alliance—Friendship) is the oldest town of Palestine, and one of the oldest of the world. Its name in the first instance was Kirjath-Arba, so named from Arba, the father of Anak, the giant (Joshua 20.1-11,15.13, 14). It was "built seven years before Zoan" (Num.

HEBRON—CAVE OF MACHPELAH.

13.22), i. e., Tanis in Egypt, and when Josephus wrote, it was 2,300 years old. In the time of Abraham it took the name of Mamre, doubtless after Mamre the Amorite, the friend and ally of Abraham (Gen. 33.19,35.27). It was at that time a walled city, for when Abraham bought the field of Machpelah, it "was in the presence of the children of Heth, before all that went in at the gate of his city" (Gen. 23.10). Damascus was a city at the same period (Eliezer of Damascus was Abraham's servant—Gen. 15.2); but whether Hebron or Damascus can claim seniority is not known.

It was here that grand old sheikh lived—the father of his people, and the friend of God (page 114). From this place the lad Joseph went forth to seek his brethren in Shechem. And here came back the sons, bringing the blood-stained garment. "And Jacob rent his clothes, and put sackcloth upon his loins, and mourned for his son many days" (Gen. 38.34).

It has witnessed many fierce struggles, notably when "Joshua went up from Eglon, and all Israel with him unto Hebron; and they fought against it; and they took it and smote it with the edge of the sword, and the king thereof and all the cities thereof, and all the souls therein; he left none remaining, but destroyed it utterly" (Joshua 10.37). Afterwards, in answer to Caleb's prayer, "Joshua blessed him, and gave unto Caleb, the son of Jephunneh, Hebron for an inheritance * * * Hebron therefore became the inheritance of Caleb unto this day * * * because that he wholly followed the Lord God of Israel" (Joshua 14.13,14). It was later made a city of refuge, unto which the pursued manslayer might flee (Joshua 20.7).

Another set of associations, equally interesting, attach to Hebron. It was here that David had his residence for seven and a half years, when he reigned over Judah

alone (2 Sam. 2.1). Here Absalom was born; and here
Abner was treacherously murdered by Joab, who "took
him aside in the gate to speak with him quietly, and
smote him there under the fifth rib, that he died * * *
and they buried Abner in Hebron; and King David himself followed the bier. And the king lifted up his voice
and wept at the grave of Abner, and all the people wept.
And the king said, Know ye not that there is a prince
and a great man fallen this day in Israel?" (2 Sam.
3.27-38).

Hither came Absalom, under the pretext of performing a vow, and "he sent spies throughout all the tribes
of Israel, saying, As soon as ye hear the sound of the
trumpet, then ye shall say Absalom reigneth in Hebron
(2 Sam. 15.10).

The other remaining events of importance are associated with places yet pointed out in Hebron, the Cave
of Machpelah, and the Pools (see below).

The modern name of Hebron is *el-Khalil*, the Friend.
It is situated in the narrow Valley of Eshcol, still
abounding with vineyards. There are no walls to the
town, but one or two somewhat superfluous gates. The
streets are dark and dirty; the houses are for the most
part substantial, and, being nearly all built of stone, and
covered with cupolas or small domes, give a curious and
interesting effect. The population has been variously
estimated, but it is probable there are about 12,000 inhabitants, many of whom are occupied in the manufacture of rings, bracelets, and many other kinds of glass
trinkets. There are no Christians in Hebron, but about
600 Jews, who still attract attention by their pale faces
and long ringlets. The Moslems of Hebron are strangely
superstitious and fanatical, and travelers should always
be upon their guard, so as not to say or do anything
which will provoke their animosity.

In the valley there are two Pools of very ancient date, which still supply the town with water. To one of these Pools, probably the southern, a story attaches. Rechab and Baanah, sons of Rimmon, thought to do King David a service by slaying Ishbosheth, the son of Saul, and therefore a rival. They brought the head of Ishbosheth to Hebron, expecting an expression of his favor, but David said unto them "As the Lord liveth who hath redeemed my soul out of all adversity, when one told me, saying, Behold, Saul is dead, thinking to have brought good tidings, I took hold of him and slew him in Ziklag, who thought that I would have given him a reward for his tidings; how much more when wicked men have slain a righteous person in his own house upon his bed? shall I not therefore now require his blood of your hand, and take you away from the earth? And David commanded his young men, and they slew them and cut off their hands and their feet and hanged them up *over the pool in Hebron*" (2 Sam. 4.9-12).

The chief interest in Hebron centers in the **Cave of Machpelah.** It is no more a cave in the midst of a field, but a mosque—a large building of massive stones, but not of a pleasing appearance. Unfortunately, we could only stand a short way off from the entrance; we dared not enter, the place being guarded with most jealous care by the Moslems. We walked by the side of the Haram, and ascended to the top of the hill and the dragoman pointed out some parts of the building, but that was all.

However, little as there may be in Hebron to see, there is much for the mind's eye to dwell upon, and no one can stand beside this spot—sacred alike to Jew, Christian, and Mohammedan—without recalling some of the most touching of Old Testament scenes.

Sarah, the beloved wife of Abraham, "died in Kirjath-

Arba, the same is Hebron, in the land of Canaan; and Abraham came to mourn for Sarah, and to weep for her. And Abraham stood up from before his dead, and spake unto the sons of Heth, saying, I am a stranger and a sojourner with you; give me a possession of a burying place with you, that I may bury my dead out of my sight." The contract with the sons of Heth was made in the gate of the city, and in the presence of all the people; and the details of the contract were such as are entered upon to this very day, as shown in "The Land and the Book."

The field, the cave, the trees in the field, all were "made sure unto Abraham for a possession." And after this "Abraham buried Sarah his wife in the cave of the field of Machpelah" (Gen. 23).

Mighty prince as Abraham was, "very rich in silver and in gold" founder of that great nation, which was to possess the land forever, this was the only spot in all Palestine that was his own, and for this he weighed out the silver unto Ephron. God "gave him none inheritance in it, no not so much as to set his foot on: yet He promised that He would give it to him for a possession, and to his seed after him, when as yet he had no child" (Acts 7.5).

In process of time "Abraham gave up the ghost, and died in a good old age, an old man, and full of years, and was gathered to his people; and his sons Isaac and Ishmael," the Jew and the Arab "buried him in the cave of Machpelah" (Gen. 25.8,9).

As Jacob lay a-dying, his thoughts turned to this quiet resting-place, and he gave a summary of its sacredness, when he charged his sons with so much explicitness saying, "I am to be gathered unto my people: bury me with my fathers in the cave that is in the field of Ephron the Hittite, in the cave that is in the field of Machpelah, which is before Mamre, in the land of Canaan, which

Abraham bought with the field of Ephron the Hittite for a possession of a burying-place. There they buried Abraham and Sarah his wife; there they buried Isaac and Rebekah his wife; and there I buried Leah" (Gen. 49.31). Probably there was never a grander funeral than that of Jacob, when Joseph, "with all the servants of Pharaoh, the elders of his house, and all the elders of the land of Egypt, and all the house of Joseph, and his brethren, and his father's house; and chariots and horsemen" carried the embalmed body from Egypt into the land of Canaan, to the cave of Machpelah.

Referring to the Cave of Machpelah, Norman Mac-Leod says:

"This is the only spot on earth which attracts to it all who possess the one creed, 'I believe in God.' The Holy Sepulchre in Jerusalem separates Moslem, Jew, and Christian; here they assemble together. The Moslem guards this place as dear and holy. The Jew from every land draws near to it with reverence and love, and his kisses have left an impress on its stones. Christians, of every kindred, and tongue, and creed, visit the spot with a reverence equally affectionate. And who lies here? a great king or conqueror? a man famous for his genius or his learning? No; but an old shepherd, who pitched his tent over 4,000 years ago among these hills, a stranger and a pilgrim in the land, and who was known only as *El-Khalil*—'the Friend.' By that blessed name Abram was known while he lived; by that name he is remembered where he lies buried; and by that name the city is called after him."

Oak of Mamre or "Abraham's Oak"

Next in interest to the Cave of Machpelah, is the **Oak of Mamre,** a journey of about half an hour. The road is somewhat difficult and slippery, being paved; vineyards abound. A gateway on the right is passed, and the grand old terebinth tree comes in view. The tree is *very* old. Tradition affirms that **Abraham's Oak** was standing here in the time of our Lord. "This tree," said a native of Jerusalem, "is over 6,000 years old." It is nearly 33 feet in girth, it has three magnificent branches which divide at about 20 feet from the ground.

I was surprised to see the tree enclosed by a stone wall, which is 8 feet high, and entered by a gate kept under lock and key.

[During the last few years more care has been taken of the sacred places; the Garden of Gethsemane, Elisha's Spring, etc., were, since my first trip with the Cook's party in 1898, more restored and greater care is being taken to preserve them.]

If this is the site of the dwelling-place of the great patriarch, it is indeed a sacred spot for here "the Lord appeared unto him in the plains of Mamre: and he sat in the tent door in the heat of the day; and he lift up his eyes and looked, and lo, three men stood by him: and when he saw them, he ran to meet them from the tent-door, and bowed himself toward the ground." Then he bade Sarah

OAK OF MAMRE, OR ABRAHAM'S OAK.

make ready the cakes upon the hearth, while he ran to the herd and fetched "a calf tender and good," and when the meal was spread Abraham received the announcement that he should have a son. It was as they rose up from this place that the Lord said, "Shall I hide from Abraham that thing which I do?" and then told him of the impending doom of Sodom and Gomorrah, which, at his intercession, the Lord said He would spare for the sake of ten righteous men (Gen. 18).

In about twenty minutes from here the road to Jerusalem is gained, and the return journey to Solomon's Pools is identical with that already described (page 108).

From Jerusalem to Jericho

My first trip, above mentioned, on a "Thos. Cook & Son Tour" was made on horseback, which was pleasant, but on the last trip we went by carriage. This carriage ride was the roughest ride of my life on that day from Jerusalem to Jericho, and as such it will long remain in my memory. The distance is about thirty miles; and the journey is now often made in a carriage. During my stay in Jerusalem I saw that the greater number of travelers chose this mode, although they sometimes had to walk distances, according to the hills they crossed, which were too steep for horses.

About seven miles from Jerusalem we reached a khân, where the water is excellent, and where travelers usually halt for their mid-day meal. There are now but few traces of the old khân, which once stood here, or of the arch covering the cistern, into which the water flows from the spring. It has been called the **Apostles' Spring,** from the legend that here the Apostles tarried on their

journeyings; and it is also supposed Christ came often
here to instruct His Apostles, and they drank of its water,
hence the name Apostles' Spring. There is little doubt
that this fountain of 'Ain-el-Haud, or 'Ain-Chot, is identical with **En-Shemesh** (Spring of the Sun), a fountain
on the boundary between Judah and Benjamin (Joshua
15.7,18.17).

After riding about six miles further, we came to an
old ruined khân. We halted, and went in this inn for
refreshments and to rest from the jolting, but very little accommodation can be obtained here. This is the
traditional scene of the parable of the **Good Samaritan**,
who rescued the certain man going *"down* from Jerusalem to Jericho, and fell, among thieves" (St. Luke
10.34).

About three hours from this khân we reached the
Dead Sea. Native Bedouin guides and armed dragomen
went with us for our protection, although there was no
cause for alarm.

The Dead Sea

is called in the Scripture the Sea of the Plain (Deut.
4.49). The Greeks named it "Dead Sea" by which name
it is now generally known, although the Arabs call it
Bahr-Lût (the Sea of Lot). According to the most reliable measurements, the sea is 46 English miles in its
greatest length, and nine and a half in the greatest
width. Its mean depth is 1,080 feet; in the south bay
the depth does not exceed eleven feet.

Lying, as it does, 1,300 feet below the level of the
Mediterranean, it is the most depressed sheet of water

GOOD SAMARITAN INN.

in the world, although it contains no living thing of any kind.

About ten miles down the Dead Sea, south of Pizgah we noticed a round topped Tell, the site on which the Castle of Machærus once stood, where John the Baptist was beheaded. "And he sent and beheaded John in the prison" (Matt. 14.10). We also saw the deep valley a little north of Machærus, called Wady Z'urka Ma'in (Callirhoe), in which are the warm baths that Herod the Great resorted to in the time of his last illness. On the east side are the mountains of Moab and Ammon over which the Israelites passed. The Mount Nebo, which is in the land of Moab, is the highest point east in a line with the north end of the sea where Moses saw the Land of Promise, and was buried in the land of Moab. I believe that it was Moses' privilege to take a view from Mount Nebo over the Promised Land, and I saw from my view, that from this high mount he must have seen nearly the whole land.

Moses was a good man and a good shepherd. He remained about forty years with the high priest Jethro, who had many flocks of sheep and many shepherds. Moses was the chieftain and herdsman of the chosen flock, and he married the priest's daughter Zipporah— the leader of the shepherdesses. He died in a good old age; he was 120 years old.

The Scripture account of the death of Moses is as follows:

"So Moses the servant of the Lord died there in the land of Moab, according to the word of the Lord. And He buried him in a valley in the land of Moab, over against Beth-peor, but no man knoweth of his sepulchre unto this day" (Deut. 34.5,6).

"The land of Moab was the native country of Ruth" (Ruth 1.16-17). "And Ruth said, Intreat me not to leave

thee, or to return from following after thee: for whither
thou goest, I will go; and where thou lodgest, I will
lodge: thy people shall be my people, and thy God my
God: Where thou diest, will I die."

History of the Dead Sea.—It was here that Lot chose
for himself a home upon its borders (Gen. 13.12). Abraham dwelt in the land of Canaan and Lot dwelled in
the cities of the plain and pitched his tent towards
Sodom. The five cities of the plain: **Sodom, Gomorrah,
Admah, Zebolim and Zoar,** were situated on the plain
and shores of the sea. Gen. 14.1 to 12 gives the account
of the battle of the four kings against five that took
place, "in the vale of Siddim, which is the Salt Sea.
* * * And the vale of Siddim was full of slime pits;
and the kings of Sodom and Gomorrah fled, and fell there";
and Lot was taken prisoner. Here were those cities of
the plain which were so full of wickedness that "the
Lord rained upon Sodom and upon Gomorrah brimstone
and fire from the Lord out of heaven; and He overthrew
those cities, and all the plain, and all the inhabitants of the
cities, and that which grew upon the ground" (Gen.
19.24,25). Here Lot's wife, looking back, became a
pillar of salt (Gen. 19.26). In Num. 34.2,12, the sea is
made one of the borders of the land, and the eastern
boundary of Judah (Joshua 15.1-5).

At the Dead Sea, there is a peculiar atmosphere which
makes one feel more than he can see. Few will care
to linger on the edge of the sea, as the heat is intense,
and one ceases to wonder that the six millions of tons
of water, which it is calculated fall daily into the sea,
need any other outlet than that which is caused by
evaporation.

From the Dead Sea to the Jordan, or rather the Pilgrims' Bathing Place, is about one hour's journey. For
some distance from the shore, the mounds and hillocks

are white with salt. The heat is overpowering, but the
sight of the green line of foliage edging the river, and
the large trees in the distance by the Bathing Place, urge
the traveler forward, and if he has been bathing in the
Dead Sea, there will be a longing desire to plunge into
the pure, fresh streams of Jordan.

The River Jordan

The Jordan forms the Waters of Merom and flows
into the Lake of Galilee, and it falls into the Dead Sea.
It takes its rise in the fork of the two ranges of Anti-
Libanus, and flows through that part of Palestine which
extends from the southern extremity of Cœle-Syria to
the Dead Sea. It crosses the rich plain of Hûleh, lying
between the last slopes of Anti-Libanus and the mountains of Galilee, and stops in the beautiful plateau of
Bascan. Here it forms the Waters of Merom (Lake
Hûleh), from whence, increased in size and force, owing
to the depression of the valley, it flows into the Lake
of Galilee. Emerging from this lake, it plunges in
twenty-seven rapids down a fall of 1,000 feet through
what is the lowest and final stage of its course.

"The only known instance of a greater fall is the
Sacramento River in California." (Stanley.) Finally,
after being enriched by the waters of Jabbok, made illustrious by Jacob's mysterious conflict, it falls into the
Dead Sea, from whence it does not emerge again.

The length of the river, in a straight line from its
source to the Dead Sea, is not more than 120 miles; its
course, however, is so remarkable that between the Lake
of Galilee and the Dead Sea, 60 miles of actual length

is increased to 200 by its corkscrew windings. The river
varies in width from 80 to 160 feet, and in depth from
five to twelve feet.

Every stage of the river is sacred with **Historical Associations.** "Lot lifted up his eyes and beheld all the
plain of Jordan, that it was well watered everywhere,"
and was "even as the garden of the Lord" (Gen. 13.10).
After the forty years' wandering, the Israelites "crossed
over it on dry ground, until all the people were passed
clean over." The passage occurred in the time of harvest, i. e., the beginning of April, when the waters were
at their highest, from the early rains, and melting
snow, "for Jordan overfloweth all his banks all the time
of harvest." "And the waters which came down from
above stood and rose up upon an heap very far from
the city of Adam, that is beside Zaretan: and those that
came down toward the sea of the plain, even the salt
sea, failed, and were cut off: and the people passed over
right against Jericho" (Joshua 3.14,17). Jacob, Gideon,
Abner, David, Absalom, and many others, crossed this
river, and here came down those two holy men, one
of whom was soon to pass into the other world. "And
Elijah took his mantle, and wrapped it together, and
smote the waters, so that they two went over on dry
ground" (2 Kings 2.8). Elisha, as he returned from
parting with his friend, taking the mantle which had
fallen from his illustrious predecessor, smote the waters,
so that they parted hither and thither, and he too passed
over on dry ground. In the waters of Jordan, Naaman
was cured of his leprosy. "And his flesh came again,
like unto the flesh of a little child, and he was clean"
(2 Kings 5).

These incidents of the Old Testament pale before the
memories of the New. Here rang out the "voice of one
crying in the wilderness. Repent ye: for the kingdom

of heaven is at hand." It has often been suggested that
the place of baptism was in the very place where Elijah,
his great forerunner, passed over; where he finished his
course, the Baptist in the spirit and power of Elias com-
menced his. "Then went out to him Jerusalem, and
all Judæa, and all the region round about Jordan; and
were baptized of him in Jordan, confessing their sins"
(Matt. 3.5,6). Most sacred of all is the memory, that
to this place came our Lord Himself, and was baptized
by John, "and, lo, the heavens were open unto Him, and
He saw the Spirit of God descending like a dove, and
lighting upon Him: and lo, a voice from heaven, saying,
This is My beloved Son, in whom I am well pleased"
(Matt. 3.13,17). Sites on the Jordan are difficult to
identify, but there seems no reason to doubt that the
passage of the Israelites, who went straight towards
Jericho; the passage of Elijah, and Elisha, who came
from Jericho; the baptism of our Lord, who was led
up by the Spirit into the wilderness to be tempted of the
devil all occurred in nearly an identical locality. Tradition has placed them at the **Pilgrims' Bathing Place.**
"Fords do not change in a river like the Jordan; roads
are never altered in the East; and this must always have
been, as it is now, the place of passage from Jericho to
Gilead * * * the Lower Ford was only used for the
passage to Moab." (Tristram.)

At Easter, the bathing-place of the Greeks is the resort of thousands of pilgrims, who come in a body from
Jerusalem to Jericho, and assemble in multitudes in the
neighborhood of Riha (page 126). Early in the morning, at a given signal, the pilgrims leave their resting-
place and proceed to the river, when old and young, rich
and poor, without much regard to propriety, plunge into
a promiscuous bath. The scene has been variously
described by many travelers, who affirm that the Greeks

attach deep religious significance to the ceremony, which is to them the source of many blessings. The Roman Catholics have a bathing-place further to the south.

Travelers who have come from the Dead Sea should make a point of bathing in the Jordan, and in fact, all travelers who can, doubtless will.

The Banks of the River, all about here, are rich in varied foliage, oleanders stand in thick masses, beautiful in early spring, with their rose-colored blossoms; a few palms and sycamore (or sycamine), fig trees, many small jujube, or thorn trees, and its largest variety the Dom tree, tall poplars, willows and tamarisks along the banks of the river; old acacias, the Salvadora persica or mustard tree, the wild olive, balsam, castor-oil plant, the false apple of Sodom, and also the osher, the true Sodom apple, the rose of Jericho, the true hyssop, colocynth, camphire, zalicornia, salsola, inula, the crimson-flowered loranthus, and a variety of others.

Here the lion in olden times had his lair, here the leopard still lurks, and wild boars find a home among the reeds. Birds abound in the neighborhood, the kingfisher, the sun-bird (remarkably like a humming-bird), turtle doves, nightingales, bulbuls, and a host of others.

The following is the extract from Mr. MacGregor's work, "Rob Roy on the Jordan":

"Jordan is the sacred stream not only of the Jew, who has 'Moses and the prophets'; of the Christian, who treasures the memories of his Master's life upon earth; of the cast-out Ishmaelite, who has dipped his wandering bloody foot in this river since the days of Hagar, but of the Moslem faithful also, wide scattered over the world, who deeply reverence the Jordan. No other river's name is known so long ago and so far away as this, which calls up a host of past memories from the Mohammedan on the plains of India, from the latest Christian

settler in the Rocky Mountains of America, and from
the Jew in every part of the globe. Nor is it only of
the past that the name of Jordan tells, for in the more
thoughtful hours of not a few, they hear it whispering
to them before, strange shadowy truths of that future
happier land that lies over the stream of death."

From the Jordan to Jericho, Bethany and Jerusalem

From the Ford of the Jordan the route is over the
level plain, and the time occupied in the journey to
Jericho is usually about two hours.

On the right, as we proceeded, I saw an old square
ruin, called Kasr el-Yehûdi, or Castle of the Jews. A
church once stood here, on the site where tradition affirms St. John the Baptist had his dwelling.

A long distance to the left there is a ruin called Kasr-
el-Hajla, the Castle of Haglah; it marks the site of **Beth-
Hogla** (Partridge House), a town of Benjamin on the
border of Judah (Joshua 15.6,18.19-21). There is a large
fountain here, and the Greeks from the Convent of Mar-.
Saba have been utilizing the ruins of the old castle for
the purpose of raising a convent. One hour from the
Jordan, we pass the **Wady-el-Kelt** (the Valley of Achor),
where Achan and his family were stoned, and in consequence of the trouble brought by him upon Israel, was
named after him. "Joshua said, Why hast thou troubled
us? the Lord shall trouble thee this day.   And all
Israel stoned him with stones, and burned them with
fire, after they had stoned them with stones. * * *
So the Lord turned from the fierceness of his anger.
Wherefore the name of that place was called, The Valley

of Achor (i. e., *trouble*) unto this day" (Joshua 7.24-26).
This ravine corresponds also with the "Brook Cherith,
which is before Jordan," where Elijah was fed by ravens
(1 Kings 17.1-7).

Rîha.—Formerly one of the most filthy spots in the
Holy Land, the town consisting of a mere heap of rubbish, of late years it has been much improved. The
Russians have built a church and a large house to accommodate their pilgrims, and numbers of Greek and
Russian monks have cultivated garden plots. When the
carriage road is completed many foreigners will, doubtless, take land in the district for garden produce. Riha
is the site of the ancient **Gilgal** and of the **modern
Jericho.** It was here that the Israelites first pitched their
camp west of the Jordan, and set up twelve stones which
they had taken from the bed of the stream (Joshua
4.19,20). Here the people celebrated their first passover in the Promised Land, and the rite of circum-
cision was performed on those who had been born in the
wilderness. "And the Lord said unto Joshua, This day
have I rolled away the reproach of Egypt from off you.
Wherefore the name of the place is called Gilgal (i. e.,
rolling) unto this day" (Joshua 5.9).

Here "the manna ceased on the morrow after they
had eaten of the old corn of the land; neither had the
children of Israel manna any more, but they did eat of
the fruit of the land of Canaan that year" (Joshua 5.12).
During all the early part of the conquest the camp remained here (Joshua 9.10). And it has been assumed,
from Joshua 14, 15, that Joshua continued to reside here.
At this place Joshua saw the vision of "a man over
against him with his sword drawn in his hand, and
Joshua went to him and said, Art thou for us or for
our adversaries? and he said, Nay, but as Captain of
the host of the Lord am I now come." And Joshua was

OUR PARTY, CAMPING AT JERICHO.

bidden "Loose thy shoe from off thy foot, for the place whereon thou standest is holy."

In later times the solemn assemblies of Samuel and Saul were celebrated here. Here the latter was made king; and when David came back from exile, the whole tribe of Judah assembled to welcome him, and to conduct him over the Jordan, after the death of Absalom (2 Kings 19.15).

Continuing our road I saw a large tower, which has been called the **House of Zacchaeus.**

From Rîha we traveled to ancient Jericho, passing through a forest, principally of thorn-trees.

Jericho

Jericho, the city of palm-trees (Deut. 34.3), and the scene of Joshua's victories, is not to be confounded with modern Jericho, or Riha. It was the chief city of ancient Canaan, and must ever have been fruitful from its contiguity to the fountain of 'Ain-es-Sultan (page 128). There is nothing to be seen at Jericho save a few mounds of ruins. The palm-trees have all gone, the mighty city is in a heap, and, but for the fountain of Elisha, and the remnants of water courses, and a few traces of ancient foundations, there would be nothing to identify it. The history of its siege and capture by Joshua will be recalled by every traveler.

"It was across yonder plain that the spies journeyed; round here went up those great walls on which Rahab had her house; over there in the mountains we seem as if we could make out the very place where the spies hid themselves; it was here that Joshua's army went round the city; and these hills echoed back the shrill blast of the trumpets which the priests blew. And when the seventh day had come, there went up from this spot the great shout of the people, mingling with the blasts of the trumpets, 'and the walls of Jericho fell down flat.' Then came that fearful panic, followed by blood, and havoc, and death. It was somewhere close by here that Rahab, with her kindred, sat with tear-dimmed eyes, and saw the smoke of the burning city ascending. And, perhaps, it was on some high standing ground near here that Joshua, in the presence of all Israel, stood, and pointing to that charred and ruined mass that had once been the strong city of Jericho, cried: 'Cursed be the man before the Lord, that riseth up and buildeth this city Jericho: he shall lay the foundation thereof in his first-born, and in his youngest son shall he set up the gates of it' (Joshua 6.26). Despite the curse, five hundred years afterwards a man was found who dared to rebuild the city, and who fulfilled the prediction by inheriting the curse (1 Kings 16.34)."—(Hodder.)

At Jericho the last days of the Prophet Elijah were spent, and from here he went forth with Elisha to cross the waters of Jordan, and to witness that strange revelation of a chariot of fire and horses of fire that parted them both asunder when Elijah went up by a whirlwind into heaven (2 Kings 2.4,5,15). Jericho was long celebrated for its beautiful groves and gardens, and these were given to Cleopatra by Anthony. Herod rebuilt the city, and erected many handsome buildings. In the time of our Lord, the Jericho visited by Him as He journeyed to Jerusalem was New Jericho. Here the two blind men were healed, and our Lord paid a visit to the house of Zacchæus (page 127).

'Ain-es-Sultan, or the Sultan's Spring, is undoubtedly the spring of water which Elisha healed, and is called

"Elisha's Fountain." The story runs thus: "And the men of the city said unto Elisha, Behold, I pray thee, the situation of this city is pleasant, as my Lord seeth: but the water is naught, and the ground barren. And he said, Bring me a new cruse, and put salt therein. And they brought it to him. And he went forth unto the spring of the waters, and cast salt in there, and said, Thus saith the Lord, I have healed these waters; there shall not be from thence any more dead or barren land. So the waters were healed unto this day, according to the saying of Elisha which he spake" (2 Kings 2.19-22). Just above the spring, the **House of Rahab** is pointed out, and some Roman pavement is still to be seen hard by.

Among the minor reminiscences of Jericho may be mentioned that it was here that Hanun, the son of Nahash, took *David's* servants, and shaved them. "Then there went certain, and told David how the men were served. * * * And the king said, Tarry at Jericho until your beards be grown, and then return" (1 Chron. 19.5). It will be remembered that this incident has given rise to a well-known English vulgarism. In Jericho Herod died, and was buried at Herodium.

The story of his last illness and death at Jericho is known to all, and how, in his dying moments while the cries of the slaughtered innocents were still being wrung out, he gave orders for all the nobles who had attended him to be put to death, "that so at least his death might be attended with universal mourning."

Not the least imposing feature in the landscape is the high, precipitous mountain called **Quarantania** (Forty Days) the traditional scene of our Lord's temptation. "And the devil, taking Him up into an high mountain, showed unto Him all the kingdoms of the world in a moment of time." Something is curious about the mountain; there hangs over it a very dark black cloud, and

our guide said: "You see there the **Mount of Temptation;** it has always a black cloud hanging over it." The
side facing the plain is perpendicular, white, and naked,
and mid-way is burrowed by holes and caverns, where
hermits used to retire for fasting and prayer, in imita-
tion of the example of our Lord. On one side of the
mount is a Greek Convent, which is fenced in by a strong
stone wall.

From Jericho to Bethany and Jerusalem

(On horseback about six hours' ride, and four by
carriage.)

Leaving Jericho, a few ruins are passed, and several
interesting valleys are crossed. The view from the top
of the Tall above 'Ain-es-Sultan is very extensive, and
is thus described by Dr. W. M. Thomson in *"The Land
and the Book"*:

"I came up to see the sun rise once more over the
eastern mountains and this impressive plain of Jericho.
Behind us on the west, tower the gray and honey-combed
cliffs of Quarantana, the Mount of Temptation; in the
foreground the green oasis, created by 'Ain-es-Sultan,
spreads to the village of Jericho; on the other side of the
river the dark mountains of Moab and of Edom bound the
eastern horizon, having the wide plain of Abel-Shittim at
their feet, and the heights of Nebo and Pisgah above. Far
away to the south the Dead Sea sleeps in its mysterious
sepulchre. Northwards stretches the valley of the Jordan,
sheltered by the lofty Kurn Surtabeh on the west, and
the noble mountains of Gilead and Bashan on the east.
This vast area of plain and mountain and river and sea

BETHANY.

is crowded with ancient sites, whose names recall many of the grandest, and some of the most sublime and appalling events in Biblical history. The mental impression of this amazing panorama will abide with you while life may last."

Continuing on our journey we passed the boundary between Judah and Benjamin, and ascended to the top of the hill; turning to the right, **Bethany** lay before us.

Before reaching Bethany one finds a Greek Chapel, where tradition says Martha met Jesus (St. John 11.20). "Then Martha, as soon as she heard that Jesus was coming, went and met Him."

Bethany

This is a little ruined, but prettily situated village, with glorious views of the distant hills of Moab, and the glittering waters of the Dead Sea, and the green line of Jordan running through the valley. Vines, figs and olives cluster on the nearer hill slopes, and the luxuriant gardens and cornfields form a very pleasant contrast to the sterility of the hills which are nearer Jerusalem.

Our guide pointed out to us the **House of Martha and Mary,** and said: "This is the house often spoken of by people throughout the world. In it lived two women of sacred fame—Martha, who was a woman of somewhat earthly thoughts, and Mary, who fixed her mind on higher things, praying and fasting and performing noble deeds."

It is a great advantage to be near the scenes of the earthly life of our Saviour, and we hold dear and very valuable the places where He once had lived. Here through the village of Bethany, we feel that more surely than in other places we are walking in the earthly footsteps of our Redeemer.

"Bethany, where the Sisters spread a thanksgiving feast to Him who raised their brother from the dead, and brought out the valuable ointment" (page 90).

I saw here an old **Tower** called the Castle of Lazarus, and near to it is the so-called **Tomb of Lazarus**, in a vault reached by descending twenty-five steps. No one should fail to read the eleventh chapter of St. John here. **Christ raised Lazarus to life,** who had been four days in the grave (St. John 11.43,44). "He cried with a loud voice, Lazarus come forth. And he that was dead came forth, bound hand and foot with graveclothes: and his face was bound about with a napkin. Jesus saith unto them, Loose him, and let him go." Bethany was frequently the **House of our Saviour** (St. Matthew 21.17), "And He left them, and went out of the city into Bethany; and He lodged there."

The site of the **House of Simon the leper,** in whose house Mary anointed Jesus, is here pointed out (St. John 12.3). "Then took Mary a pound of ointment of spikenard, very costly, and anointed the feet of Jesus, and wiped His feet with her hair."

The colt on which Jesus made His triumphal entry into Jerusalem was here (St. Mark 11.1, 2). "And when they came nigh to Jerusalem into Bethpage and Bethany, at the Mount of Olives, He sendeth forth two of His disciples, and saith unto them, Go your way into the village over against you: and as soon as ye be entered into it ye shall find a colt tied, whereon never man sat; loose him and bring him." Jesus blessed His disciples here (St. Luke 24.50). "And He led them out as far as to Bethany, and He lifted up His hands, and blessed them."

After passing Bethany, at the bend of the road before coming in sight of Jerusalem, is the place where the multitude met Jesus (St. Matthew 21.9).   In order to continue the tour we come to the point where Zion is first seen, where Jesus wept over the city (St. Luke 19.41-44).

As soon as we returned to Jerusalem we went to our hotel and asked for heat, as there is great difference in the temperature between Jericho and Jerusalem.   One of the Arab servants, who wore a red Turkish fez, brought a coal holder into the reception hall to start a fire, and as we sat near, warming ourselves, an ancient story was brought to mind.   We thought of that time, centuries past, when soldiers, coming from the cold air of the hills, sought warmth and shelter within the court of the Palace of Caiaphas, and of how Peter, trembling with cold and fear, came among them as they sat by their fires.

In ancient times Palestine was known as the land of milk and honey, and at the hotel we ate of delicious honey and drank the milk of goats which browse on the hills.   These goats are of a variety which I have never seen elsewhere; their hair being long and brown, and their ears so long that they reach to the ground.

Before leaving Jerusalem my wife and I decided to take a last view of the sacred places in the vicinity and with this object made a tour round the walls, outside of the city, which walk can be accomplished in an hour and twenty minutes.

From Jerusalem to Samaria, Nazareth, Mt. Tabor, Cana of Galilee, Horns of Hattin, Sea of Galilee, Tiberias, Capernaum, Mt. Hermon, Damascus, Ba'albek, Mt. Lebanon, Beyrout,

From Jerusalem to Samaria

Leaving Jerusalem by the Damascus Gate, the road leads by the Tombs of the Kings and the hill Scopus. Looking back from this point, the view of Jerusalem is remarkably fine, the most wonderful and interesting in all the world, and usually—as it is most frequently the traveler's last view of the **Holy City**—leaves an indelible impression on the mind. Nearly every traveler has described his emotions on leaving Jerusalem, and in the vast majority of instances his last view has been obtained from this spot. Here Crusaders, pilgrims of all ages, devotees of all phases of religion, have experienced emotion; and the place has therefore a sacredness of its own. If it be possible, every traveler should get his first view of Jerusalem from the Mount of Olives, as you come from Bethany, and the last view from this hill of Scopus.

Passing over a broad plain, and taking a northerly direction, we saw on the left the village of **Shâfât,** with part of a ruined church or tower, and cisterns hewn in the rock. Shâfât is identified by Mr. Porter as the site of the ancient **Nob.** About two miles beyond is **Gibeah,** the home of Saul; three miles further north is **Ramah,** the birthplace of Samuel, and three miles beyond that, El-Bîreh, the ancient **Beeroth.** Tradition says El-Bîreh is the place where the **Holy Family** stopped at the close of the first day after leaving Jerusalem, and turned back to the city, when they discovered that the child Jesus was not with them.

There are fine views from the hill of Tuleil-el-Fûl, a short distance further on. Shâfât, which is the site of the ancient Nob, is a priestly city of Benjamin, the place where the Tabernacle and Ark were stationed in the time of Saul, to which David fled (1 Sam. 21.4). Abimelech, the priest, having received Saul as a refugee, was informed against by Doeg the Edomite, and Nob was smitten with the edge of the sword in consequence (1 Sam. 22.9-19). **Tuliel-el-Fûl** (the little Hill of Beans) is, without doubt, the **Gibeah** of Saul, the native place of the first King of Israel, and the seat of government during the greater part of his reign (1 Sam. 10.26,14.2). This is the place where the seven descendants of Saul were hanged by the Amorites, and the scene of one of the most touching stories of motherly love on record. Two of her sons were amongst those who were thus slain, and they "were put to death in the days of harvest, in the first days in the beginning of barley harvest. And Rizpah the daughter of Aiah took sackcloth, and spread it for her upon the rock, from the beginning of harvest until water dropped upon them out of heaven, and suffered neither the birds of the air to rest on them by day, nor the beasts of the field by night" (2 Sam. 21.10). Thus, for six months, and those the hottest of the year, the sorrowing woman watched the bodies of her sons, and proved the truth of the saying, "Love is stronger than death." The site of the city is now a dreary and desolate waste, and the ruins are not of importance.

The next site of any interest on the road is a hill on the right, where is the village of **El-Ram**, identical with **Ramah** of Benjamin—from whence there is a fine view. It was between Gibeon and Beeroth (Joshua 18.25). Here was the scene of that terrible story of the Levite (Judges 19) which brought about the great war with the Benjamites. It is not improbable that here was fulfilled the prophecy, "A voice was heard in Rama, lamentation and bitter weeping" (Jer. 31.15; Matt. 2.17,18).

Proceeding on our journey, we pass a ruined village on the ridge of a hill, supposed to be the site of Ataroth-addar, on the borders of Benjamin and Ephraim (Joshua 16.5). In little more than half an hour we reach **El-Bîreh**, a village with about 800 inhabitants, an excellent spring of water, ruins of reservoirs, and an old khân.

On a piece of high ground are the remains of a church, which was built by the Crusaders, but the tradition dates only from the sixteenth century. El-Bireh is identified with the ancient **Beeroth** (wells)—one of the four Hivite or Gibeonite cities that made the league with Joshua (Joshua 9.17). It was allotted to Benjamin (Joshua 18.25), and is mentioned as the birth-place of one of David's mighty men "Naharai, the Beerothite" (2 Sam. 23.37).

El-Bireh is the place where the Holy Family stopped (page 134). The journey from El-Bireh to Bethel occupies only about half an hour, and the principal things to be noted on the way are the reservoir in a cavern, and a fountain, 'Ain-el-Akabah. Then, in five minutes,

Bethel, or Beitîn

Bethel is now but a poor village on a hill, with wretched huts, and about 500 inhabitants. Everywhere round about I saw traces of ancient materials, even for the building of the hovels of the people. There are the remains of a tower in the highest part of the village, and near these the walls of a church.

An old cistern, constructed of solid masonry, is in a

grass-grown field hard by, and as the "wells of water" in Palestine are always surrounded with memorable associations, the traveler is advised to resort thither in order to picture the scenes of Bethel's ancient glory. For the mere view, however, the ruins of the tower on the top of the hill present a wider field.

Bethel was the place where Abraham reared an altar, and called upon the name of the Lord, who had just given this land to him, and to his seed after him, forever. From here he went into Egypt, and fell into temptation, dishonoring God before the heathen king, who sent him away out of the land. "And he went on his journeys from the south, even to Bethel, unto the place where his tent had been at the beginning, between Bethel and Hai; unto the place of the altar which he had made there at the first: and there Abram called on the name of the Lord" (Gen. 13.3-4).

Here Jacob, weary with his forty miles' journey, and away from home and kindred, "took of the stones of that place, and put them for his pillows, and lay down on that place to sleep" (Gen. 28.11).

Here he saw the vision—the wondrous vision of angels ascending and descending the mystic ladder, and when he awoke he made the solemn vow which consecrated him to the service of God.

The name of this place was Luz, but Jacob said, "This is none other than the house of God, and this is the gate of heaven, and he called the name of that place Bethel" (i. e., the House of God). When Jeroboam sought to wean the hearts of the people from the service of God at Jerusalem, he set up here the golden calf, against which the prophet of Judah was sent to cry in the name of the Lord, and, to confirm his mission by a sign, the altar was rent in pieces by invisible hands, and its ashes poured out. Jeroboam stretched out his hand against the prophet, and it was withered until it was restored at the intercession of the prophet. Bethel, the House of God was changed into Bethaven, the House of Idols, until at length the prophecy, uttered by the man of Judah, was fulfilled in the person of Josiah, who utterly destroyed every memorial of the idolatrous worship established by Jeroboam, and spared nothing in the city save the sepulchre of the man of God from Judah, who cried that day against the altar. For the whole of this dramatic story, see 1 Kings 12,13; 2 Kings 23.15-20.

Here, or hereabouts, "there came forth two she bears out of the wood, and tare forty-and-two children"—little children who said to Elisha, "Go up, thou bald head."

After the Babylonish Captivity, Bethel was inhabited again by the Benjamites. In later times it was captured by Vespasian, and finally dwindled down to its present insignificance.

A short distance from Bethel is **Ai,** celebrated as the scene of Joshua's victory.

Bethel presents an interesting subject to the devotional student. Here was the House of God, the place of altars, and of visions, and vows. Here arose the alien sanctuary, with its idolatrous altar, and here may be seen God's protest against false worship. "The high places also of Avon, the sin of Israel, shall be destroyed; the thorn and the thistle shall come up on their altars" (Hosea 10.8). "For thus saith the Lord, Seek ye Me and ye shall live, but seek not Bethel. * * * Bethel shall come to naught" (Amos 5.4,5).

Somewhat curiously, Bethel is not mentioned in any part of the New Testament.

Leaving Bethel we enter at first upon rather a rough road, but in an hour, after ascending a hill, we reach the most fertile regions of Palestine, abounding with vineyards and orchards, and still bearing everywhere the signs of the blessing of Ephraim (Deut. 33.14,15). To the left is the village of 'Ain Yebrûd, one of the most fertile spots in the fertile land of Ephraim, but the road to it is a hard one to travel.

By and by we see Jifna, and 'Ain Sinia, and then the village of Yebrûd. One or two ruins are passed, one of them called the Kasr-el-Berdawil, supposed to mean the Castle of Baldwin. We are now in an exquisite valley, or glen, called the Wady-el-Haramîyeh (i. e., Glen of the Robbers). At 'Ain-el-Haramiyeh, the Robbers' Fountain, the water is remarkably good and the scenery exceedingly picturesque, but the reputation of the place is bad to the last degree, as its name implies. Leaving the glen with its caverns and cisterns, and profusion of ferns where the water drips down the cliff, we enter in a more open valley which is as romantic as any in Palestine, and soon arrive at Sinjîl.

Shiloh, Arabic *Seilûn*, is now one large heap of ruins, and the first thought of the traveler, as he beholds the large mound covered with masses of rubbish, enormous stones, and pieces of broken columns, will be the particularly graphic fulfillment of the prophecy of Jeremiah, who used it as a type of the destruction which should fall upon the house of the Lord in Jerusalem.

"Go ye now unto my place which was in Shiloh, where I set my name at the first, and *see what I did to it* for the wickedness of my people Israel. And now, because ye have done all these works, saith the Lord, and 1 spake unto you, rising up early and speaking, but ye heard not; and I called ye, but ye answered not; therefore will I do unto this house, which is called by My name, wherein ye trust, and unto the place which I gave to you and to your fathers, as I have done to Shiloh" (Jer. 7.12-14). "I will make this house like

Shiloh, and will make this city a curse to all the nations of the earth" (Jer. 26.6).

The history of Shiloh was remarkable. I viewed the ruins with the keenest interest, being satisfied that there can be no shadow of doubt that Seilûn is the site of Shiloh.

Here Joshua divided the land among the tribes, and here the Tabernacle was reared (Joshua 18). Around the ruins of the ancient well "the daughters of *Shiloh*" danced in the yearly festival (Judges 21.19-23). Here dwelt Eli, and to this place Hannah came yearly to the sacrifice, bringing with her the "little coat" for the boy Samuel, who ministered before the Lord (1 Sam. 1). Many eventful scenes occurred here—the sins of the sons of Eli, the sudden death of the old man, as he heard in one breath of the desolation of his own house, and the desolation of the house of God. With the loss of the Ark, Shiloh lost all; it was taken by the Philistines and never returned, and from that time the city is seldom even mentioned. Ahijah, the prophet, dwelt here, and hither in disguise came the wife of Jeroboam to learn the doom of that sinful house (1 Kings 14).

Among the ruins I saw the remains of an ancient church. On the entablature of the doorway is sculptured an amphora between two wreaths. The front of the ruins is pyramidal, and four columns yet remain erect. Other fragments, denoting former greatness, are strewn about.

The plain in the spring-time presents a green and well cultivated appearance, thus forming a striking contrast to the site on which Shiloh stands.

Crossing now the cultivated fields, we descend to the Wady-el-Lubbân, and by and by reach a fountain of excellent water, beside the ruined **Khân el-Lubbân**. This is supposed to be the ancient **Lebonah**, and if so it estab-

lishes the position of Shiloh. "Behold there is a feast
of the Lord in Shiloh yearly, which is on the north side
of Bethel, on the east side of the highway that goeth up
from Bethel to Shechem, and on the south of Lebonah"
(Judges 21.19).

We are now on a much better road, passing the village of Es-Sâwiyeh on the left, and in a few minutes
more the khân of the same name. We rest for a while
under a large oak-tree, and then descend by a rather
sharp road to the Wady Yetma, then travel uphill to a
bleak plateau, where a splendid view greets the traveler.
Stretched before us is the great plain, surrounded by the
mountains of Samaria. Before us on the left is Gerizim,
and beyond that Ebal, while far away to the north is
the snow-clad Hermon. Everywhere there is fertility,
and although so many ages have passed since the dying
patriarch gave his blessing on Ephraim, the "good
things" remain, even to the olive and the corn, the fig
and the vine, the fruitful bough by a well, and blessings
prevailing unto the utmost bounds of the everlasting
hills (Gen. 49.26).

Instead of proceeding by the road on the left, which
leads direct to Nâbulus, we were advised to take the
road on the right, which leads to Jacob's Well.

The plain is beautiful, level, and the horses that had
for the past few days been picking their way over stony
places, were probably as glad as the riders to have a
good canter here, and as in Palestine the opportunities
are so rare, it is well to make the most of them.

Jacob's Well

is a very sacred spot. Its authenticity has never been
doubted. There can be no question that it was here that
our Saviour sat. Around us are the corn-fields to which
He pointed when He said, "Lift up your eyes, and look
on the fields, for they are white already to harvest"
(John 4.35). Over there to the right is the parcel of
ground that Jacob gave to his son Joseph. There is the
opening between the two hills, with just a glimpse of
Shechem beyond; there on the left is Gerizim, to which
the woman of Samaria pointed, as she said, "Our fathers
worshipped in this mountain." "The well is not what we
understand by that name. It is not a spring of water
bubbling up from the earth, nor is it reached by excavation. It is a shaft cut in the living rock, about nine feet
in diameter, and now upwards of seventy feet deep. As
an immense quantity of rubbish has fallen into it, the
original depth must have been much greater, probably
twice what it is now. It was therefore intended by its
first engineer as a reservoir, rather than as a means of
reaching a spring. Then again, if any wall, as some
suppose, once surrounded its mouth, on which the traveler could rest, it is now gone. The mouth is funnel-
shaped, and its sides are formed by the rubbish of old
buildings, a church having once been erected over it.
But we can descend this funnel and enter a cave, as it
were, a few feet below the surface, which is the remains
of a small dome that once covered the mouth. Descend-

142

WATER CARRIER.

ing a few feet, we perceive in the floor an aperture partly
covered by a flat stone, and leaving sufficient space
through which we can look into darkness."—(MacLeod.)

"It was pleasant to sit here and think of what might,
perhaps, have been some of the thoughts of the Saviour
as He sat thus on the well, being wearied with His
journey. Perhaps He was thinking of Abraham, who
built his first altar in the land in this opening of the
plain (Gen. 12.6), or of Jacob, whose only possession in
the Land of Promise was here (33.19), and even then,
bought and paid for as it had been, it was taken from
him by the Amorites; but he reconquered it from them.
'I took it out of the hand of the Amorite with my sword
and my bow,' said the dying old man (Gen. 48.22), and
left it to Joseph, who, long years afterwards, gave com-
mandment concerning his bones, which were brought
from Egypt and buried here (Joshua 24.32). Perhaps
Christ thought of Joseph, wandering in that very field
in search of his brethren (Gen. 37.15), and saw, in the
persecution of the brethren, and the final victory of the
beloved son, one of the divine pictures of the past, testifying of Himself; or, perhaps, His thoughts were dwelling upon that first gathering of all Israel, when first they
came into the land, and there was set before them a
blessing and a curse. Perhaps He heard again the 'Amen'
of the people, as the curses were uttered from Ebal; or
saw the smile of joy as the blessings on hearth and home,
and land and business, were pronounced from Gerizim,
and 'sighed deeply' as He grieved for the hardness of
the hearts of that favored people, who had gone in the
way of evil, and brought upon them all the full letter
of awful doom pronounced upon the disobedient (see
Deut. 11.28, 29, 30; Joshua 8.30,35). No wonder that,
in the midst of associations such as these, He should
say, 'I have meat to eat that you know not of.' Before

Him was unrolled, throughout that land, the volume of the ages, and in every page He read the 'things concerning Himself.' "—(Hodder.)

It is but a short and pleasant journey from Jacob's Well to Nâbulus.

Nâbulus or Shechem

Nâbulus, corrupted from Neapolis, or Flavia Neapolis, is the name given to the town in commemoration of its restoration by Titus Flavius Vespasian. Anciently it was Sichem or Shechem, and in the New Testament is called Sychar and Sychem. When Abraham arrived here the Canaanite was then in the land (Gen. 12.6). In Jacob's time Shechem was a Hivite city, under the governorship of Hamor, the father of Shechem (Gen. 33.18, 19). The city was captured by Simon and Levi, who murdered all the male inhabitants and brought upon themselves the dying malediction of their father Jacob. "Cursed be their anger, for it was fierce, and their wrath, for it was cruel" (Gen. 34.49.5-7). Somewhere about here Joseph was seized by his brethren, and sold to the Ishmaelites (Gen. 27.); here, too, he was buried (page 143).

When the land was divided, Shechem fell to the lot of Ephraim (Joshua 20.7), but subsequently became a Levite city of refuge (Chron. 6.67).

Here all Israel assembled in the time of Joshua. After the death of Solomon, Rehoboam and Jeroboam met here, and the result was the division of the kingdom, Shechem being made the seat of the new government under Jeroboam (1 Kings 12.1-25). It became the center of Samaritan worship after the return from captivity. Our Lord tarried here for two days, "and many believed on Him for the saying of the woman which testified, He told me all that ever I did. So when the Samaritans were come unto Him, they besought Him that He would tarry with them: and He abode there two days. And many more believed because of His own word; and said unto the woman, Now we believe, not because of thy saying: for we have heard Him ourselves, and know that this is indeed the Christ, the Saviour of the world" (John 4.39-42).

During the history of the Crusaders Nâbulus suffered considerably. From that time to the present, the people have been noted for their extreme exclusiveness, rigid adherence to their traditions, and for their quarrelsome spirit.

Nâbulus contains about 12,000 inhabitants, of whom about a hundred and fifty are Samaritans, the rest of the population being made up of Jews and Christians of the Greek, Catholic and Protestant Churches. The streets are narrow, and not over clean. The houses are well built, of stone, crowned with cupolas. The people have a bad reputation for their discourteous treatment of strangers, and until recently Christian visitors were greeted with cries of *Nozrani!* (Nazarene!), accompanied by pelting of stones. The staple trade of the town is the manufacture of soap; the **Bazaars** are well stocked, and present the usual aspect of Eastern bazaars.

For mere sightseers, the curiosities of the town are not extensive. There is a large **Mosque,** which was once a Crusader's Church, consecrated to St. John, and probably belonging to the Knights of St. John. A curious legend attaches to a smaller mosque in the southwest part of the town (once a **Samaritan Synagogue**)—namely, that it stands on the site where Jacob sat, when his sons spread before him the blood-stained coat of Joseph (see page 111). There is nothing of interest in Shechem, however, so great as the Samaritan people, whose quarter is in the southwestern part of the town. For nearly three thousand years they have lived here, bound up in their own prejudices, separate from all other people of the earth, having their own Pentateuch, and retaining their own forms of service, sacrifice and worship. While empires and dynasties have risen and passed away, these people still hold their own, and retain all the marked peculiarities of their race.

The **History of the Samaritans** it is impossible to even outline in the limited space of this work. The word "Samaritan" only occurs once in the Old Testament (2 Kings 17.29), and then in a sense wholly different from that in which it is used in the New. The origin of the people is doubtful, but it is supposed by some that they were Assyrians; and by others that they were a remnant of the Israelitish people who were not carried away into captivity; and by others that they were colonists from various foreign nations who took possession during the Captivity. The account given in 2 Kings 17.24 is as follows: "The King of Assyria brought men from Babylon, and from Cuthah, and from Ava, and from Hamath, and from Sepharvaim, and placed them in the cities of Samaria instead of the children of Israel: and they possessed Samaria, and dwelt in the cities thereof." When the Jews returned from Babylon, the Samaritans—who, after instruction, "feared the Lord, but served their own gods"—desired to assist Zerubbabel in rebuilding the Temple, but were repulsed, and then, their anger aroused, hostility to the Jew and his worship burst forth. They determined to rival Jersualem by a temple of their own, and built one on Mount Gerizim, in the days of Manasseh. Of course, the animosity was now increased be-

SAMARITAN HIGH PRIEST, AND PENTATEUCH ROLL AT SHECHEM
—SUPPOSED WRITING OF ABISHUA, GREAT GRANDSON OF AARON.

tween the rival races. It became a sin on either side to
extend the rites of hospitality, and the feeling expressed
by the woman of Samaria was an index of the feeling
which for ages existed between the two races, and, to
some extent, exists to-day. "How is it that thou, being
a Jew, asketh drink of me, which am a woman of Samaria? for the Jew. have no dealings with the Samaritans."

The Samaritans believe in one God; they expect the
Advent of the Messiah; they believe "in the resurrection of the body, and the life of the world to come."
They only acknowledge the authority of the Pentateuch
in the Old Testament writings; and their literature,
which is exceedingly meagre, consists principally of
hymns and commentaries, and a one-sided history of
their own nation. They observe the Jewish Sabbath,
and all the principal feasts which were ordained by
Moses—to wit, the Passover (page 149), the Feast of
Atonement, the Feast of Tabernacles, and others.

In the **Samaritan Quarter,** in the southwest part of
the town, is their synagogue—a small, oblong chamber;
uncomfortably modern. Divine service is performed in
the Samaritan dialect, the high-priest—whose office is
hereditary, and whose salary consists of tithes—leading
the prayers and praises, after a manner not always agreeable to the taste of those who hear.

The great curiosity of the synagogue is the celebrated
Samaritan Codex of the Pentateuch—a document which
has given rise to a vast amount of discussion. It has
been affirmed that it was written in the time of Moses
and again, that it was the production of a grandson of
Aaron. That it is a curious, interesting and ancient
MS., there is no doubt; nor is there much doubt that it
is little, if any, older than the Christian era. Some cap-
tious critics have affirmed that it is not more than three

hundred years old, but it must be borne in mind that the Samaritan MS. is rarely shown to ordinary travelers for fear of wearing it out by over-much use, and that a comparatively modern copy has to do duty for the old one.

The **situation of Nâbulus,** every traveler will admit, is very beautiful, and from every point of view the prospect is pleasing. Beautiful foliage, luxuriant vegetation, terraces upon terraces of fruit, gardens, orchards, babbling brooks, white-topped houses, pleasant hills, and deep valleys. There is everything that can be crowded together in a limited space to make up a perfect picture.

It is in the midst of beautiful scenes in nature that perhaps the distress at witnessing personal misfortune is most experienced, and no traveler can stay an hour in Nâbulus without hearing the plaintive cry of the **Lepers.** Unhappily, these poor creatures intrude their misfortunes before the gaze of the stranger, who is often sorely tried at witnessing the distorted faces and wasting limbs, and to hear the horrible and husky wail peculiar to themselves. These miserable folk are identical in their habits and appearances with those who were formerly found at the Zion Gate in Jerusalem (page 71). They dwell apart, and marry only amongst themselves. Their children, until the age of ten or eleven, are as pleasing in appearance as other children, but after that age the deadly taint exhibits itself, and they, too, dwell apart in the leper community.

Mount Gerizim

No traveler should omit the ascent of Gerizim (the Mount of Blessing). The ascent is steep, especially towards the top, and the fear of committing cruelty to animals will probably prevent kind-hearted folk from using the horses which have laboriously brought them to Shechem, as they can procure fresh ones, or donkeys, in the town. Leaving Shechem, from the usual camping ground on the west we pass through the valley, and, soon after commencing the ascent, reach the spring Ras-el-'Ain; then the ascent becomes steeper, a large plateau is reached, and turning to the left, the open space, where the Samaritans encamp during the Feast of the Passover, is seen.

In case the traveler should have no opportunity of witnessing this interesting Festival, he will read with great interest the following description: "On the tenth of the month the sacrificial lambs are bought. These may be either kids of goats or lambs; the latter being generally, if not at all times, chosen. They must be a year old, males, and 'without blemish.' The number must be according to the number of persons who are likely to be able to keep the feast. At present they are five or six, as the case may be. During the following days, which are days of preparation, these are carefully kept, and cleanly washed—a kind of purification to fit them for the paschal service; a rite, in all probability,

always observed in connection with the temple service
(John 5.1). Early on the morning of the fourteenth day,
the whole community, with few exceptions, close their
dwellings in the city, and clamber up Mount Gerizim;
and on the top of this, their most sacred mountain, pitch
their tents in a circular form, there to celebrate the most
national of all their solemnities. I, and the friends who
had joined me at Jerusalem, had pitched our tent in the
valley, at the foot of Gerizim; and on the morning of
the 4th of May, we clambered up the mountain.

"On reaching the encampment, friendly voices greeted
us from several tents, and having visited those best
known to us, we rested for a while with our friend Amram. Presently we took a stroll up to the temple ruins,
and from thence had a perfect view of the interesting
scene. The tents, ten in number, were arranged in a
kind of circle, to face the highest point of the mountain,
where their ancient temple formerly stood, but is now
lying in ruins.

"Within a radius of a few hundred yards from the
place where I stood, clustered all the spots which make
Gerizim to them the most sacred mountain, the house of
God. * * * About half past ten, the officials went
forth to kindle the fire to roast the lambs. For this
purpose a circular pit is sunk in the earth, about six feet
deep, and three feet in diameter, and built around with
loose stones. In this a fire made of dry heather, and
briars, etc., was kindled, during which time Yacub stood
upon a large stone, and offered up a prayer suited for
the occasion. Another fire was then kindled in a kind
of sunken trough, close by the platform, where the service was to be performed. Over this two caldrons, full
of water, were placed, and a short prayer offered * * *
There were forty-eight adults, besides women and children, the women and the little ones remaining in the

tents. The congregation were in their ordinary dress,
with the exception of the two officers, and two or three
of the elders, who were dressed in their white robes, as
in the synagogue.

"A carpet was laid on the ground near the boiling
caldrons, where Yacub stood to read the service, assisted
by some of the elders—all turning their faces towards
the site of the temple. Six lambs now made their appearance, in the custody of five young men who drove
them. These young men were dressed in blue robes of
unbleached calico, having their loins girded. Yacub,
whilst repeating the service, stood on a large stone in
front of the people, with his face towards them. * * *
At mid-day the service had reached the place where the
account of the paschal sacrifice is introduced: 'And the
whole assembly of the congregation of Israel shall kill
it in the evening' (Exod. 12.6), when, in an instant, one
of the lambs was thrown on its back by the blue-clad
young men, and the *shochet,* one of their number, with
his flashing knife, did the murderous work with rapidity.
I stood close by, on purpose to see whether he would
conform to the rabbinical rules; but the work was done
so quickly that I could observe nothing more than that
he made two cuts. The other lambs were despatched
in the same manner. Whilst the six were thus lying
together, with their blood streaming from them, and in
their last convulsive struggles, the young *shochetim*
dipped their fingers in the blood, and marked a spot on
the foreheads and noses of the children. The same was
done to some of the females; but to none of the male adults.
The whole male congregation now came up close to the
reader; they embraced and kissed one another, in con-
gratulation that the lambs of their redemption had been
slain.

"Next came the fleecing of the lambs—the service

still continuing. The young men now carefully poured
the boiling water over them, and plucked off their fleeces.
Each lamb was then lifted up, with its head downwards,
to drain off the remaining blood. The right fore-legs,
which belonged to the priest, were removed and placed
on the wood, already laid for the purpose, together with
the entrails, and salt added, and then burnt; but the
liver was carefully replaced.

"The inside being sprinkled with salt, and the ham-
strings carefully removed, the next process was that of
spitting. For this purpose, they had a long pole, which
was thrust through from head to tail, near the bottom
of which was a transverse peg, to prevent the body from
slipping off. The lambs were now carried to the oven,
which was by this time well heated. Into this they were
carefully lowered, so that the sacrifices might not be
defiled by coming into contact with the oven itself. This
accomplished, a hurdle, prepared for the purpose, was
placed over the mouth of the oven, well covered with
moistened earth, to prevent any of the heat escaping.
By this time it was about two o'clock, and this part of
the service was ended.

"At sunset the service was recommenced. All the
male population, with the lads, assembled around the
oven. A large copper dish, filled with unleavened cakes
and bitter herbs rolled up together, was held by Phineas
Ben Isaac, nephew of the priest; when, presently, all
being assembled, he distributed them among the congregation. The hurdle was then removed, and the lambs
drawn up one by one; but, unfortunately, one fell off
the spit, and was taken up with difficulty. Their appearance was anything but inviting, they being burnt
as black as ebony. Carpets were spread ready to receive
them; they were then removed to the platform where
the service was read. Being strewn over with bitter

herbs, the congregation stood in two files, the lambs being in a line between them. Most of the adults had now a kind of robe around the waist, and staves in their hands, and all had their shoes on. 'Thus shall ye eat it; with your loins girded, your shoes on your feet, and your staff in your hand' (Exod. 12.11). The service was now performed by Amram, which continued for about fifteen minutes; and when he had repeated the blessing, the congregation at once stooped, and, as if in haste and hunger, tore away the blackened masses piecemeal with their fingers, carrying portions to the females and little ones in the tents. In less than ten minutes the whole, with the exception of a few frag-ments, had disappeared. These were gathered and placed on the hurdle, and the area carefully examined, every crumb picked up, together with the bones, and all burnt over a fire kindled for the purpose in a trough, where the water had been boiled. 'And ye shall let nothing of it remain until the morning; and that which remaineth of it until the morning ye shall burn it with fire' (Exod. 12.10). Whilst the flames were blazing and consuming the remnant of the paschal lambs, the people returned cheerfully to their tents."—(Mills.)

In about ten minutes from the camping place, the **Summit of Gerizim** is reached. It is nearly three thou-sand feet above the level of the sea, and consists of a large open space, at one end of which are the ruins of a church or castle; the walls are thick and of hewn stones, probably belonging to a period anterior to "the castle" which was built by Emperor Justinian. There is also a Moslem *wely*, a reservoir, and a few other ruins, and part of a pavement. Near to the castle are some massive stones, identified by a legend with the twelve stones brought up from the Jordan and erected at Gilgal as a memorial (page 126).

Near here is a piece of rock, which is stated to have been the altar of their great temple; and as the Samaritans arrogate to themselves the Jewish history, they say that Abraham offered up Isaac here, that Jacob had the vision of the heavenly ladder here, etc., etc. It is *the* sacred place of the Samaritans; towards it they always turn in prayer; they never approach it but with uncovered feet, and here they celebrate their most sacred festival (see page 149). The view from the table-land on the summit is exquisite. In the far west are the waters of the Mediterranean; in the north, the snowy top of Hermon, partly intercepted by Mount Ebal; below, to the east, is the fruitful plain of Makhna, and beyond, the Mountains of Gilead.

Mount Ebal, on the north side of the valley of Nâbulus, is celebrated for its view, which is finer than that from Gerizim. The ascent is by no means difficult; and the view of the mountains of Galilee, from Carmel on the left to Gilboa on the right, with Tabor and Safed, and a host of memorable places, is well worth the fatigue, if time permits.

From either mountain, the scene recorded in Joshua 8.33,34, will be recalled with interest, for in the valley of Nâbulus and on the hillsides, the tribes of Israel were assembled, while the Levites lifted up their voices, and pronounced from Gerizim blessings upon the obedient, and from Ebal cursings upon the rebellious. "And all Israel, and their elders, and officers, and their judges, stood on this side the ark and on that side, before the priests and the Levites, which bare the ark of the covenant of the Lord, as well the stranger, as he that was born among them; half of them over against Mount Gerizim, and half of them over against Mount Ebal; as Moses the servant of the Lord had commanded before, that they should bless the people of Israel. And after-

wards Joshua read all the words of the law, the blessings and the cursings, according to all that is written
in the book of the law." It is a curious fact that, owing
to the formation of the hills, they form, as it were, a
natural sounding-board; and many travelers have affirmed that, standing in the plain, they have been able
to hear distinctly the utterances of friends stationed on
the mountains, who have gone there to test the accuracy
of the statements of Moses and Joshua (Deut. 27.11-13).

The journey from Nâbulus to Samaria is through the
beautiful valley, where every variety of vegetation will
be seen. There are many brooks and streams of water,
which divide in this valley; those on the east flowing
to the Jordan, and those on the west to the Mediterranean.

Several pleasant-looking villages, mostly on hills, we
noticed on either hand; and in the distance, standing
alone in the valley, we saw the Hill of Sebastiyeh.

Samaria,

or Sebastiyeh, from Sebaste, the name given it by Herod,
is now nothing more than a small, dirty village, surrounded by hedges of cactus and ruins, speaking elo-
quently of the former grandeur through their contrast
with the present desolation. As at Shiloh (page 139), so
here, the burden of prophecy comes to the mind of the
traveler as he looks upon the desolate scene, and hears
the word of the Lord, "Samaria shall become desolate,
for she hath rebelled against her God" (Hosea 13.16).
"I will make Samaria as a heap of the field, and as a
plantings of a vineyard, and I will pour down the stones

thereof into the valley, and I will discover the foundations thereof" (Micah 1.6).

The city was built by Omri, King of Israel, and became the capital of the ten tribes until the Captivity. It took its name from Shemer, from whom the hill was purchased. It was the center of idolatrous worship. Here Ahab built the Temple of Baal, which was destroyed by Jehu. "He reared up an altar for Baal in the house of Baal, which he had built in Samaria. And Ahab made a grove, and Ahab did more to provoke the Lord God of Israel than all the Kings of Israel that were before him" (1 Kings 16.32,33).

During his reign the city was besieged by the Syrians; but Ben-hadad of Damascus was defeated by a small band of Israelites. The story of the siege of Samaria, as recorded in 2 Kings 6.24-33, will be recalled by every traveler as he walks through the ruins, and those striking incidents (1) of the compact between the starving women: "Give thy son, that we may eat him to day, and we will eat my son to morrow"; and (2) of the "four leprous men who sat at the entering in of the gate, and said one to another, Why sit we here until we die?" and then entering into the city, found "there was no man there, neither voice of man," for the Syrians had fled in terror, even for their life. Again and again the city was besieged, and ultimately it was captured by the Assyrians, in the reign of Hosea, the inhabitants being carried into captivity (2 Kings 17.24). After various revivals, the city was taken by John Hyrcanus. Pompey restored it to Syria, and Augustus gave it to Herod the Great, who rebuilt it with great magnificence, and named it *Sebaste* (the Greek translation of the Latin name Augustus).

It was to this Samaria that St. Philip came, preaching the gospel. "Then Philip went down to the city of

Samaria, and preached Christ unto them. And the people with one accord gave heed unto those things which Philip spake, hearing and seeing the miracles which he did. * * * And there was great joy in that city" (Acts 8.5-8). As Nâbulus grew in importance, Sebaste began to decay, and finally declined until it has become as a heap of ruins. "Woe to the crown of pride * * * whose glorious beauty is a fading flower" (Isaiah 28.1).

In walking through the village of Sebastiyeh, we noticed how traces of ancient buildings are to be found, even built up into the most miserable hovels, so that in some bare and filthy rooms, we saw slender shafts of columns, or curiously wrought capitals, intended once to please the eyes of kings. There are many interesting (if genuine) sites pointed out, such as the gate where the lepers sat; the palace of Ahab, the temple of Herod, the old market, etc. The principal sight is the **Church of St. John,** a very picturesque ruin. It was a Christian church, but has now become a mosque. There are traces of a nave with two aisles. On the walls are crosses of the Knights of St. John. In the center of an open court, there is a dome over the traditional sepulchre of St. John the Baptist. In order to enter the tomb, a number of steps have to be descended, and here is pointed out the tomb of the Baptist, the tomb of Obadiah, besides one or two others. There is also shown a massive stone door, four feet high, said to be the actual door of St. John's prison. It will be remembered that Josephus states that St. John was beheaded in the castle of Machærus, on the Dead Sea (page 119). St. Jerome is the first writer who refers to the tradition that St. John was buried here. The tomb is called by the Arabs Neby Yahya.

The **Colonnade,** or "Street of the Columns," many of which are monoliths, extending round the hill side, are more interesting than anything else to be seen in Samaria. "The remains of the ancient city consist mainly of colonnades, which certainly date back to the time of the Herods, and perhaps many of the columns are much older. * * * The grand colonnade runs along the south side of the hill, down a broad terrace, which descends rapidly towards the present village. The number of columns, whole or broken, along this line, is nearly *one hundred,* and many others lie scattered about on lower terraces. They are of different sizes, and quite irregularly arranged, but when perfect it must have been a splendid colonnade. The entire hill is covered with rubbish, indicating the existence and repeated destruction of a large city."—(The Land and the Book.)

From Samaria to Nazareth

Leaving Samaria we descend the hill, where are the columns, and enter the Valley of Barley, and in about half an hour arrive at the pleasant village of **Burka,** where there are some fine old olive trees, under which travelers often camp. When the top of the hill is reached, a very fine view bursts on the sight—an extensive plain studded with villages. Descending into the valley, a village named Jeb'a—supposed to be a Gibeah, of which there were many—is seen, and here the short-cut from Nâbulus joins the main road.

After passing through a pleasant glen, a broad valley is entered. On a hill to the left stands the fortress of *Sânûr,* besieged in 1830 by the Pasha of Acre, and destroyed by Ibrahim Pasha.

Ascending a rough and rocky road, a grand and impressive view is seen, and here is the Plain of Esdrælon, with all its crowding memorial-places round about, and in the far distance stands the white-robed Hermon. From here, too, are seen the ruins of **Dothan,** whither Joseph came seeking his brethren, and the Ishmaelites, passing by, bought him, at the instigation of Reuben, for thirty pieces of silver (Gen. 37.).

It was at Dothan that Elisha the prophet tarried during the time that Ben-hadad was marching towards Samaria. Fearing the prophet of Israel, who, it was said, revealed to the king of Israel all his movements, Ben-hadad sent a host to compass the city of Dothan with horses and chariots. The servant of the man of God feared, but Elisha said, "Fear not: for they that be with us are more than they that be with them. And Elisha prayed, and said, Lord, I pray thee, open his eyes, that he may see. And the Lord opened the eyes of the young man; and he saw: and, behold, the mountain"—probably the mountain on which the traveler stands—"was full of horses and chariots of fire round about Elisha." Then were the Syrians smitten with blindness, and were led into Samaria (2 Kings 6.13-23).

A rocky, slippery descent into the valley, where the village Kubâtiyeh is seen, and then through a narrow glen, famous in past days as a stronghold of robbers, and we arrived at the prosperous and beautifully situated village of Jenin.

Jenîn is, without doubt, the En-gannim (Fountain of Gardens) of Scripture. It was a town on the border of Issachar, allotted to the Gershonite Levites (Joshua 19.21-29). The village has about 3,000 inhabitants, its "gardens" are exceedingly fruitful, and the "spring" still supplies the people with excellent water.

Josephus mentions this town, under the name of Ginea, as one of the boundaries between Samaria and Galilee.

The Plain of Esdraelon,

on the edge of which Jenin stands, is the Plain of Jezreel, the Hebrew form of the Greek Esdrælon (Joshua 17.16); called also Esdra-Elon (Judith 7.3). In Zech. 12.11, it is called the Valley of Megiddo; and by the Apostle John, Armageddon—*i. e.*, the city of Megiddo (Rev. 16.16). This plain stretches from the Mediterranean between Akka on the north and the head of Carmel on the south, across central Palestine, with an average width of ten or twelve miles, to the river Jordan on the east. It forms a depression between the mountains of Lebanon on the north, and those of Samaria on the south. It is, with but few slight undulations here and there, a level plain, exceedingly rich, and capable of a high state of cultivation. Unfortunately, plundering Arabs make the place so insecure, that gigantic thistles and wildernesses of weeds take the place of profitable cultivation; and nowhere, except in some of the eastern branches of the plain, is there a single dwelling.

Looking across the plain, as we leave Jenin, we have on the north Tabor and Little Hermon (the former not visible until some distance has been traversed); on the east, the mountains of Gilboa, terminating in the ridge, where the story of the death of Saul and Jonathan is localized; on the south the mountains of Samaria. This plain has been a battlefield from the days of Barak to Napoleon. Warriors out of every nation which is under heaven have pitched their tents in the Plain of Esdrælon, and have beheld the different banners of their nations wet with the dews of Tabor and of Hermon.—(Dr. Clarke.)

Esdrælon was the frontier of Zebulun (Deut. 33.18), and the special portion of Issachar. Here Barak, descending from Mount Tabor, and ten thousand men after him, discomfited Sisera, whose defeat was owing, in great measure, to his having been drawn to the river Kishon—a river which drains the plain into the Mediterranean. "The river of Kishon swept them away; that ancient river, the river Kishon" (Judges 5.21). Here Josiah the king came to fight with Necho, the king of Egypt, and received his death-wound (2 Chron. 35.20-25). From generation to generation Esdrælon was the scene of plunder and of war; the Canaanites who, under Jabin, King of Canaan, had nine hundred chariots of iron, which could work fearful mischief on the level plain, mightily oppressed the children of Israel for twenty years (Judges 4.3). Then the Midianites prevailed against Israel; "and so it was when Israel had sown, that the Midianites came up, and the Amalekites and the children of the East, even they came up against them, * * * and destroyed the increase of the earth * * * for they came up with their cattle and their tents, and they came as grasshoppers for multitude" (Judges 6.1-6). It was held for a long time by the Philistines, who had a fortress at Bethshean (1 Sam. 29, 31), and the Syrians frequently swept through the plain with their armies (1 Kings 20.26).

From Jenin to Haifa, Acre, and Mount Carmel, takes about thirteen hours.

As we proceed on our journey towards Nazareth, the different points of interest will be more particularly mentioned.

There is a direct caravan route across the plain, but it is exceedingly uninteresting. We shall therefore take the route which contains the most interest.

After leaving Jenin, several very small villages are passed. Our dragoman pointed out, on the left, the village of Ta'-annuk, the Taanach of Joshua 17.11, and Megiddo, Judges 5.17. Passing under the bare mountains of Gilboa (in Arabic, *Jebel Fakû'a*), we notice on the right a Moslem shrine called Neby Mezâr, and soon afterwards reach Zer'in, the ancient Jezreel. Zer'in is a wretched little village, surrounded by heaps of rubbish, and burrowed with innumerable holes, which are used as storehouses, where produce and other things are garnered out of reach of the thievish Bedouins. The view is wide and interesting, commanding the Plain of Esdrælon as far as to Carmel on the one side, and the Jordan Valley on the other. On the north of Zer'in is that part of the plain known as the Valley of Jezreel.

Associations crowd upon us. Here was the palace of Ahab, not a trace of which remains. Looking down upon the fields, we saw the one which Ahab coveted of Naboth. "Give me thy vineyard, that I may have it for a garden of herbs, because it is near unto my house." The traveler will read with interest 1 Kings 21—how Naboth clave to the inheritance of his fathers, how Ahab fretted over the one crook in his lot, how Jezebel proceeded with her wicked machinations, how Elijah the Tishbite came down with the messages of wrath, and how Jezebel, as "she painted her face, and tired her head, and looked out at a window," was thrown out on to the stone paving of the court, and the wild pariah dogs came as the instruments of destruction, fulfilling the saying, "Thus saith the Lord, in the place where dogs licked the blood of Naboth, shall dogs lick thy blood, even thine." A writer has well said, "God has written in letters of blood across that field of Naboth, 'Beware of covetousness!'"

It was "in the portion of Naboth the Jezreelite" that Jehu, who came up the valley "driving furiously," put Jehoram to death. And here Ahaziah was slain (2 Kings 9.15-26, 30-37). It was in the valley of Jezreel that Gideon gained his victory over the Midianites (see page 164).

From Zer'in there is a road goes direct to Nazareth, but the only place of interest passed is Fûleh. We took the more interesting route.

Fûleh, which can be seen from Zer'in, means "a bean," but what the name has to do with the place appears uncertain. In the time of the Crusaders, there was a castle belonging to the Templars and Knights of St. John standing here, which was taken by Saladin; the ruins on the mount are the remains of this castle. In 1799 it was the scene of a great battle between the French and the Turks, known in history as the battle of Mount Tabor. Kleber, with a handful of men—about 1,500—kept the Syrian host, consisting of about 25,000, at bay for about six hours; he was nearly being worsted, when Napoleon, with a yet smaller handful of men—about 600—came to his aid, and the Turks, thinking a large army was upon them, fled, and the French arms were victorious.

Instead of going direct across the valley to Shunem, we decided to make a short *détour* to the east, in order to visit 'Ain Jâlud, or "the Fountain of Jezreel," sometimes called the "Fountain of Gideon." The water of the fountain is clear as crystal, issuing from a rocky cavern. It was here that Gideon was encamped against the Midianites, and at this fountain each of the three hundred picked men lapped "the water with his tongue, as a dog lappeth. * * * And the Lord said unto Gid-

eon, By the three hundred men that lapped, will I save
you, and deliver the Midianites into thine hand!" While
"the Midianites and the Amalekites and all the children
of the east lay along in the valley like grasshoppers for
multitude, and their camels without number, as the sand
by the sea-side for multitude"—slept,—Gideon, who had
received a vision in a dream, arose, and dividing "the
three hundred men into three companies, he put a trumpet in every man's hand, with empty pitchers, and lamps
within the pitchers." By-and-by, a cry rang through
the startled air, "The sword of the Lord and of Gideon!"

Then every man broke his pitcher and the light
streamed forth, "and they stood every man in his place
round about the camp, and all the host ran, and cried,
and fled." In the confusion every man's hand was
against his fellow in the vanquished camp, the dead and
dying strewed the valley, while the remnant fled down
the valley of the Jordan; and so the sword of the Lord
and of Gideon prevailed.

On this very ground where Gideon, "strong in the
Lord, and in the power of his might," had gathered his
armies around him, close by the Fountain of Jezreel,
Saul pitched his camp, while the Philistines were encamped over there at Shunem; the armies were in full
sight of each other, and between them lay the plain we
were shortly to cross. "And when Saul saw the host of
the Philistines, he was afraid, and his heart greatly
trembled." In the midst of his camp he was alone.
Samuel, on whose advice he could have relied, was dead;
David, whose prowess helped him out of an apparently
greater difficulty than the one before him, estranged. He
had no one to whom he could go, he had by his sins
estranged himself from God; yet he sought the Urim and
Thummim, that ancient oracle, but it was dumb. "The
Lord answered him not by dreams, nor by Urim, nor

by prophets." Suspense was unbearable; if he could not get an answer from heaven, could he from hell? In his distress and anxiety he bade a messenger go seek a woman that had a familiar spirit—the very class of imposters his own decree, instigated by Samuel, had banished from the land.

The messenger returned, and told him of the Witch of Endor, and, under the cover of darkness, he set out, with two attendants, to consult her. It was a dangerous journey; but what was the outward peril compared with "the horror of great darkness" upon his soul? The road which Saul took can be unmistakably traced from here. He must have crossed the plain, gone round the left flank of the enemy, ascended the ridge of Little Hermon, and then have gone down a rather steep descent to Endor. There God answered him; there the Father of Spirits permitted his servant Samuel to speak with him from the dead; there the strong delusion which believed a lie was used by the Almighty as an instrument to his own ends; there the proud and reckless Saul, the godless Man yet God's anointed, heard his death like a sound of a bell rung from the spirit world, and his doom pronounced: "To morrow shalt thou and thy sons be with Me: the Lord also shall deliver the host of Israel into the hands of the Philistines."

Back through the darkness to his camp, and at the breaking of the day to arms! The Philistines poured down the valley, the Israelites were forced up the hillslopes of Gilboa. "And the battle went sore against Saul, and the archers hit him; and he was sore wounded of the archers." Terrified with a great soul-terror, seeking death but finding it not, and dreading to be made the sport and mock of the Philistines if captured, he begged his armor-bearer to thrust him through. Even this last boon was denied. Fixing his sword into the blood-stained ground, with the energy of despair he fell upon it—and so perished the King of Israel.—(Hodder.)

In Mr. Stanley's book, this vivid passage occurs: "The Philistines instantly drove the Israelites up the slopes of Gilboa, and however widely the route may have carried the mass of the fugitives down the valley to the Jordan, the thick of the fight must have been on the heights themselves, for it was 'on Mount Gilboa' that the wild Amalekite, wandering, like his modern countrymen, over the upland waste 'chanced' to see the dying king, and 'on **Mount Gilboa**' the corpses of Saul and his three sons were found by the Philistines the next day. So truly has David caught the peculiarity and position of the scene, which he had himself visited only a few days before the battle (1 Sam. 29.2). 'The beauty of Israel is slain in the *high places.* * * * O Jonathan, thou wast slain in *thine high places,*' as though the bitterness of death and defeat were aggravated by being not in the broad and hostile plain, but on their own familiar and friendly mountains. And with an equally striking touch of truth, as the image of that bare and bleak and jagged ridge rose before him, with its one green strip of table-land, where, probably, the last struggle was fought —the more bare and bleak from its unusual contrast with the fruitful plain from which it springs—he broke out into the pathetic strain: 'Ye mountains of Gilboa, let there be no dew, neither let there be rain upon you, *nor fields of offerings:* for there the shield of the mighty is vilely cast away, the shield of Saul, as though he had not been anointed with oil' " (2 Sam. 1.19-27).

When the Philistines came to strip the slain on Mount Gilboa, after the fatal battle; "they found Saul and his three sons, fallen on Mount Gilboa, and they cut off his head and stripped off his armour, and sent unto the land of the Philistines round about to publish it in the house of their idols and among the people. And they put his armour in the house of Ashtaroth: *and they fastened his body to the wall of Beth-shan"* (1 Sam. 31.7-10).

Leaving the Fountain of Jezreel, we make our way across the plain, which is very swampy, after recent rains, to the little village of **Sûlem**, the **Shunem** of Scripture, a town of Issachar. The village is a great contrast to many which we have seen in Palestine. It has a tidier and more well-to-do aspect. A short distance from the village, which is surrounded with a thick hedge of the prickly pear, there is an enchanting grove of orange, lemon, and citron trees, with pleasant grassy knolls, and a spring of delicious water. Hither the village maidens, bearing pitchers of water, generally follow the traveler, and there is no pleasanter spot in which to rest and be thankful.

Shunem is where the Philistines had their encampment when they waged war with Saul (page 164). Another incident will be recalled with interest. Here the Shunamite woman showed hospitality to the Prophet Elisha, and seeing that he was a holy man, she said to her husband, "Let us make a little chamber, I pray thee, on the wall, and let us set for him there a bed, and a table, and a stool, and a candlestick, and it shall be when he cometh to us he shall turn in thither." Her heart was made glad by a promise—which at first she did not believe would be fulfilled—but by and by her home was made glad by the music of a child's voice. "And when the child was grown, it fell on a day that he went out to his father to the reapers. And he said unto his father, My head, my head. And he said to a lad, Carry him to his mother. And when he had taken him and brought him to his mother, he sat on her knees till noon, and then died. And she went up and laid him on the bed of the man of God, and went out." Then swift as anxious love could bear her, she drove across the plain to tell her trouble to the man of God at Mount Carmel. Elisha returned with her, went up unto the room of death, "and he lay upon the child and put his mouth upon his mouth, and his eyes upon his eyes, and his hands upon his hands, and he stretched himself upon the child; and the flesh of the child waxed warm" (2 Kings 4.8-37).

Skirting the hill in a northeasterly direction, a journey of less than a hour brings the traveler to **Nain.** It is a shabby little village, with many rubbish-heaps and traces of ruins around; but it stands in a good situation beside the hill, and commands a fine view of the Galilean hills. Above the town are holes in the face of the hill, doubtless rock tombs. The interest attaching to Nain cannot be told better than in the simple language of the Gospel narrative, which has made the spot memorable forever.

"And it came to pass, the day after, that He went into a city called Nain; and many of His disciples went with Him, and much people. Now when He came nigh to the gate of the city, behold, there was a dead man carried out, the only son of his mother, and she was a widow: and much people of the city was with her. And when the Lord saw her, He had compassion on her, and said unto her, Weep not. And He came and touched the bier; and they that bare him stood still. And He said, Young man, I say unto thee Arise. And he that was dead sat up, and began to speak. And He delivered him to his mother" (Luke 7.11-15).

"What has Nineveh or Babylon been to the world in comparison with Nain? And this is the wonder constantly suggested by the insignificant villages of Palestine, that their names have become parts, as it were, of the deepest experiences of the noblest persons of every land and every age."—(Mac Leod.)

From Nain to Endor is a ride of about fifty minutes.

There is nothing to be seen at **Endor** (Arabic, *Endûr*) —which was at one time a town of Manasseh, and, as late as the time of Eusebius, a large village—except the caves; and these are the principal objects of attraction It has been supposed that this place was the scene of the death of Jabin and Sisera. "Do unto them as unto the Midianites, as to Sisera as to Jabin, at the brook Kishon, which perished at Endor; they became as dung for the earth."

The **Cave** in which the Witch of Endor dwelt was pointed out to the traveler; hither came Saul the night before the fatal battle (page 165). He asked that whosoever he should name should be brought before him. "Then said the woman, Whom shall I bring up unto thee? And he said, Bring me up Samuel. And when the woman saw Samuel, she cried with a loud voice: and the woman spake to Saul, saying, Why hast thou deceived me? for thou art Saul. And the king said unto her, Be not afraid: for what sawest thou? And the woman said unto Saul, I saw gods ascending out of the earth. And he said unto her, What form is he of? And she said, An old man cometh up; and he is covered with a mantle. And Saul perceived that it was Samuel, and he stooped with his face to the ground, and bowed himself" (1 Sam. 28.11-14). Then followed the prophecy of Samuel, declaring his death on the morrow, on hearing which the terrified and conscience-stricken man swooned away.

Leaving Shunem, we descend into the plain, and have before us **Mount Tabor.** It is a beautiful hill, somewhat in the shape of a sugar-loaf, flattened at the top; it stands alone on the plain, except where a narrow, and in some places imperceptible ridge unites it to the hills of Galilee; its height from the plain is about 1,350 feet, and from the sea level over 2,000 feet. The history of Mount Tabor may be briefly summarized. It was here that Deborah commanded Barak to gather his army, "So Barak went down from Mount Tabor, and ten thousand men after him. And the Lord discomfited Sisera, and all his chariots, and all his host, with the edge of the sword before Barak" (Judges 4.14,15).

Tabor is referred to in the wars of Gideon (Judges 8.18,19), and in the Psalms and elsewhere it is mentioned in poetical and figurative allusions. "The north and the south Thou hast created them: Tabor and Hermon shall rejoice in Thy name" (Psalm 89.12). The Prophet Jeremiah, when telling how Nebuchadnezzar, king of Babylon, should come and smite the land of Egypt, utters these words: "As I live, saith the King, whose name is the Lord of hosts, surely as Tabor is among the mountains, and as Carmel by the sea, so shall He come" (Jer. 46.18, see also Hosea 5.1). The mountain is not referred to by name in the New Testament; but tradition was universally believed for many centuries, that this was none other than the Holy Mount, the scene of our **Lord's Transfiguration.**

As we approach the high hill on which Nazareth stands, we notice the village of Iksâl, supposed to be Chisloth-Tabor (flank of Tabor), on the boundary of Zebulun (Joshua 19.12). Where the rocks are barren and precipitous, a worthless tradition has given the name Mount of Precipitation, alleging that it was from here the people of Nazareth sought to cast the Saviour down headlong. Now commences a sharp ascent, through glens and gullies, over steep and rugged places, where the well-tried Syrian horses pick their way with marvelous sagacity, and at length the town of Nazareth is seen, and we enter it in about twenty minutes after sighting it.

Bonfils.

NAZARETH.

Nazareth

Nazareth is not named in the Old Testament. Its history dates from the time of Christ, and after that time
until that of Constantine, it appears to have attracted
little, if any, attention.

The derivation of the name Nazareth is exceedingly
doubtful. Some have affirmed that it is taken from a
Hebrew word *Nasar*—a twig. In the time of our
Lord, the name of Nazarene was used as a term of con-
tempt, and to this day the boys in Nâbulus and other
towns of Palestine still greet the Christian traveler
with cries of *Nozrãni!* (Nazarene!) The modern name
of the town is En-Nâsirah.

Since the events which rendered Nazareth famous
occurred (page 173), the town has gone through a variety
of vicissitudes. Until the time of Constantine its inhabitants were Samaritan Jews; then it passed into the
hands of Greek, Frank and Arab. The Crusaders built
churches here, which the Turks in later years plundered
and destroyed. Christians of different sorts endeavored
to establish themselves here, but were never positively
successful until about the eighteenth century. Among
the remarkable things in the modern history of Nazareth
are the circumstances that Napoleon supped here on
the night of the Battle of Tabor, and that a plot was
laid here by Pasha Jezzâr to murder all the Christians
in his dominions as soon as the French had evacuated;

his bloodthirsty scheme, however, was thwarted by Sir Sydney Smith, the English admiral.

It is very difficult to arrive at a correct estimate of the population of any place under Turkish rule. Roughly there are about five to six thousand inhabitants in Nazareth. Of these, certainly more than half belong to the orthodox Greek Church, then follow United Greeks, Catholics, Protestants, Maronites, and various other Christian communities, making up four-fifths of the population, the rest being Moslems.

Nazareth is still, as probably it was at the time of the angel's visit, a large village or small town, situated upon the slope of one of the hills which enclose a hollow or valley. This vale, which is about a mile long by half a mile broad, resembles a circular basin shut in by mountains. It is a pleasant spot, and one might almost think that the fifteen mountains which enclose it had risen around to guard it from intrusion. It is a rich and beautiful field in the midst of barren mountains, abounding in fig trees, and showing many small gardens with hedges of the prickly pear, while the rich, dense grass affords an abundant and refreshing pasture. The town stands at the left, or western, end of the vale, and commands a view over the whole of its beautiful extent. The town itself, as beheld from the valley or from the enclosing hill, is very picturesque, backed as it is by high cliffs and approached from under the shade of spreading oaks; with substantial-looking houses of stone, the square, massive walls of the church and monastery, and the graceful minarets of two mosques, interspersed with, and here and there overtopped by the tall, spiral forms of the dark green cypress tree.—(Dr. Kitto.)

The people are celebrated for their kindness and courteousness. They are a better class of people altogether than is to be met with in any town in Palestine; their dwellings are cleaner and their habits altogether different from those met with elsewhere.

Nazareth was the residence of Joseph and Mary, and the scene of the Annunciation. "The angel Gabriel was sent from God unto a city of Galilee, named Nazareth, to a virgin espoused to a man whose name was Joseph" (Luke 1.26,27). From here Joseph went up to Bethlehem, "to be taxed with Mary his espoused wife" (2.4). After the return from Egypt, this was the home of our Lord until He entered upon His public ministry, "that it might be fulfilled which was spoken by the prophet, He shall be called a Nazarene" (Matt. 2.23). When entering upon His public ministry, "Jesus came from Nazareth of Galilee, and was baptized of John in Jordan" (Matt. 3.13). Afterwards, "He came to Nazareth where He had been brought up" (Luke 4.16). And then His fellow townsfolk sought to kill Him. They "rose up, and thrust Him out of the city, and led Him unto the brow of the hill whereon their city was built, that they might cast Him down headlong. But He passing through the midst of them went His way, and came down to Capernaum" (4.29-31). Henceforth Capernaum was His own city and it does not appear that He ever again visited the scene of His boyhood and early manhood, although He must have seen it in the distance, as He passed by on His journey to Jerusalem.

The Catholic Convent is one of the most interesting places in Nazareth; it is enclosed within high walls, and contains the **Church of the Annunciation.** The high altar is dedicated to the angel Gabriel, and is approached by marble steps on either side. Several fairly good pictures adorn the church, which has also a good organ. Below the altar is the crypt, from which one descends by a broad flight of fifteen marble steps, leading into the Chapel of the Angels, and this again leads by two steps into the

Chapel of the Annunciation. "Where the angel told her that she should have a Son called Jesus." *Here a marble altar stands with an inscription,*

"Hic verbum caro factum est"
("Here the Word was made flesh")

On the right and left are columns, marking the places where the angel and Mary stood; the latter is only a broken column, and tradition says it was thus destroyed by enemies who sought to destroy the church, and were miraculously prevented.

A doorway leads from this chapel into the **Chapel of Joseph,** and from this is a stairway leading into the **Kitchen of the Virgin**—a mere cave, the mouth of which is pointed out as being the chimney.

It will be remembered that the **Holy House of Nazareth** is not really here, but at Loreto, in Italy. It is stated that when the basilica erected by the pious care of the Empress Helena over the Virgin's house at Nazareth fell into decay, the Casa Santa, or Holy House, was brought (by angels) to a spot between Fiume and Tersato, on the coast of Dalmatia, where it rested three years. Thence it was again carried off by angels in the night to the ground of a certain widow Laureta (whence Loreto). A church was erected there, and round it a village soon gathered, to which Pope Sixtus V. accorded the privileges of a town. Half a million pilgrims resort there annually; in fact, it is one of the most frequented sanctuaries of Christendom.

The **Workshop of Joseph** is in the possession of the Catholics. Only a small portion of the wall is claimed to be the original workshop.

The **Table of Christ,** where, it is said, He met with His disciples, and dined both before and after the resurrection, was pointed out, and also the **Synagogue,** in the possession of the United Greeks, where He is said to have taught (page 173).

To the minds of most, there are two places in Nazareth sacred with the holiest associations. The first is the Fountain of the Virgin; and the second, the *Wely* at the top of the hill behind Nazareth.

The **Fountain of the Virgin** is a plentiful spring of water issuing from three mouths. Above it, the Orthodox Greeks have their own special Church of the Annunciation. The scene at the fountain is always interesting, and especially so in the evening, when it is thoroughly Eastern. Here the village maidens, in their white robes and bright head-dresses, assemble, and bear away well-filled pitchers on their heads. There can be no reasonable doubt that she who was "blessed among women" would often come here, perhaps carrying the infant Saviour in just the same fashion as we saw modern mothers of Nazareth carrying their children; and no doubt many a time our Saviour, as He came past here on His way home from rambling on the hills, would tarry to quench His thirst at this very stream whose waters the traveler may drink today as a cup of blessing.

The **Wely Sim'ân,** on the top of the high hill behind Nazareth, commands one of the best views in the country, and comprehends nearly all Palestine. "At a glance you seem to take in the whole land, and the first thought that strikes you is that this must have been a favorite resort of the Saviour, and if so, He must have had constantly spread before Him the great library of Biblical story." On the north of Hermon; on the south, the mountains round about Jerusalem; on the east, the mountains of Gilead; on the other side Jordan; and on the west, the great sea (Mediterranean). Looking across to the west, we were able to make out the beautiful Bay of Acre; the ridge running out into the sea is Mount Carmel, crowned with its convent. Southward are the mountains of Samaria; southeast, the hills around Jenin; eastward, the mountains of Gilead; and between them and us lies the magnificent Plain of Esdrælon, covered with its rich green carpet, and threaded with the silver line of "that ancient river, the river Kishon." Northward the view culminates in glory, as Hermon, like a great wall of white crystal, stands out against the blue sky, with the Galilean hills below it, and everywhere round that region; scenery varied and picturesque.

The details of this picture I greatly appreciated, and could distinguish those places I had recently visited, Jenin, Jezreel, Gilboa, Little Hermon, Nain, Tabor, and, just below my feet, the picturesque town of Nazareth, rich in gardens and flowers, and fruitful fields and plenteous orchards.

There is in Nazareth a good field for Christian work, and there are one or two places which will perhaps be visited with pleasure. The **Protestant Church** is a handsome building, standing in a very commanding position; it is capable of holding about five hundred people, and the clergyman is a man full of benevolence, and has won his way to hearts of many of the people. He labors under the arrangements of the Church Missionary Society.

The **Girls' Orphanage** in Nazareth, established by the Society for Promoting Female Education in the East, is in a flourishing state, and if every traveler would withhold a little undeserved backsheesh, and give it to this deserving institution, he would be helping on a good cause.

From Nazareth to Tiberias

The first village we passed was **Reineh,** without any historical association (so far as is known), and nothing to attract attention save an old sarcophagus, richly ornamented, which stands by the roadside, and is used as the common water-trough of the village. A little further on we saw, on the top of a hill, the village of **Meshhad,** supposed to correspond with **Gath-hepher,** a town on the border of Zebulun, and the birthplace of the Prophet "Jonah, the son of Amittai, the prophet, which was of Gath-hepher" (2 Kings 14.25). Tradition locates the tomb of Jonah here, and his shrine is the *Wely* on the hill.

Kefr Kenna, an insignificant village with about 500 inhabitants, was for centuries considered to be the **Cana of Galilee** where Christ performed His first miracle, at the Marriage Feast (John 2.1); where He healed the nobleman's son, who lay sick at Capernaum (4.46-54); and where Nathaniel "the disciple in whom there was no guile," was born (21.2). There is a Greek church in the latter village, where, of course, one of the actual waterpots used at the Marriage Feast was pointed out.

After passing Kefr Kenna, we enter a really beautiful plain, and pass two or three villages which have no associations of interest attaching to them, and then reach **Lûbieh,** where there are a few ruins and rock tombs in the hill slopes.

We have now on our left, rising up out of a fruitful plain, a curiously-shaped hill, having on its summit two peaks or horns, from which it derives its name of **Kurûn Hattîn**, or **Horns of Hattîn**, where Christ preached the Sermon on the Mount (Matt. 5.6,7). In the time of the Crusaders this place first came into notice as a holy place, the Latins having decided that it was the **Mount of Beatitudes**, where our Lord preached the Sermon on the Mount. Another tradition makes this also the scene of the Feeding of the Five Thousand (Matt. 14.15-21).

"And there followed Him great multitudes of people from Galilee, and from Decapolis, and from Jerusalem, and from Judæa, and from beyond Jordan." (Compare Matt. 4.25,5.1 with Luke 6.17-20.)

"And when it was evening, His disciples came to Him, saying, This is a desert place, and the time is now past; send the multitude away, that they may go into the villages, and buy themselves victuals. But Jesus said unto them, They need not depart; give ye them to eat. And they say unto Him, We have here but five loaves, and two fishes. He said, Bring them hither to Me. And He commanded the multitude to sit down on the grass, and took the five loaves, and the two fishes, and looking up to heaven, He blessed, and brake, and gave the loaves to His disciples, and the disciples to the multitude. And they did all eat, and were filled: and they took up of the fragments that remained twelve baskets full."

Near here Saladin, in July, 1187, defeated the Crusaders. It was their last struggle. At nightfall they gathered together by the Horns of Hattîn; Guy of Lusignan, with Raynald of Chatillon, the Grandmaster of the Knights Templars, and the Bishop of Lydda, bearing the Holy Cross. That day, however, was the triumph of the Moslem, and the power of the Crusaders in the Holy Land was broken forever. King Guy was taken prisoner; Chatillon, to whom Saladin owed many a bitter grudge, was slain; and all the mighty army of noble knights, whose deeds of valor have a charm for all, and have been faithfully chronicled by Michaud, were slain or taken prisoners.

Proceeding towards Tiberias, we enter upon a ridge of hills, beautifully level, and soon come to a spot where a **magnificent view** is obtained of the sea of Galilee and its surroundings. This view has been described by everyone who has visited the Holy Land with great praise.

In the foreground are the steeply sloping and well clothed banks leading down to the lake, which lies as in a basin a thousand feet or more below. The whole of the lake, from Tiberias on the right, away to Capernaum on the left, is distinctly seen. Across the lake, rise the irregular hills, sloping down more or less precipitously to the water's edge; they are bare and barren, it is true, but rich and varied in tone and tint. Behind them are the mountains of Galilee, and away to the north Hermon rises, and, always grand, seems from here more magnificent than ever. Thus the view consists of verdant slopes, a deep blue lake of considerable extent, with hills rising from it. It is impossible, however, to separate from these matter-of-fact details the spirit and inspiration of the scene; for yonder was the dwelling-place of Christ. Upon those waters He trod; those waves listened to His voice, and obeyed; over there, on the left, He preached the Sermon on the Mount; from one of those plateaus above the rugged hills the swine fell into the lake. Every place the eye rests upon is holy ground, for it is associated with some most sacred scenes in the life of the Master; everywhere the Gospel is written upon this divinely illuminated page of Nature, and the very air seems full of the echo of His words.

The descent to Tiberias is very steep, and we were struck with the change in temperature, reminding us of the descent into the Valley of the Jordan. The views are interesting, especially as the old walled town of Tiberias makes a picturesque foreground to the scenery of the lake.

Tiberias

Tiberias is not mentioned in the New Testament, and there is no reason to believe that it was ever visited by our Lord. The only reference to it is in one or two verses speaking of the "**Sea of Galilee,** which is the Sea of Tiberias" (John 6.1,21.1). It was built by Herod Antipas, A. D. 20, and was dedicated by him to the Emperor Tiberias. It is doubtful whether there ever was an older city on this site. It soon became the chief city of the province of Galilee; many handsome buildings adorned it, amongst them a royal palace and an amphitheater. After the destruction of Jerusalem it became the seat of the Jews. In the second century the Sanhedrim was removed here from Sepphoris, and for a long time it was noted for its Rabbinical School. Here the Mishna and Masorah, the principal traditional works of the Jews, were published. Its subsequent history is merely that of captures by Persians, Arabs, and Crusaders.

The modern town of Tiberias does not occupy so large a space as the ancient; it is partially surrounded by a wall, which was shaken and nearly destroyed in the great

TIBERIAS AND THE SEA OF GALILEE.

earthquake of 1837, when half the people of the town
perished. It abounds with fleas, and has become a
proverb in this respect. The population is over three
thousand, nearly two thousand of whom are Jews. They
are easily recognized; many of them wear immense
black hats, many wear their hair in ringlets, and nearly
all look pale and effeminate. Like the Jews in Jerusalem, they for the most part live on charity. They belong to two sects, the Ashkenazim and the Sephardim;
the former have five synagogues, and the latter two.

The **Catholic Church, or Monastery,** close by the lake
dates from the time of the Crusades, and was rebuilt in
1869.

The Jews' Burial Ground is a spot universally sacred
to Jews, as here are buried the most celebrated of their
modern men, including Jochanan, and the celebrated
philosopher Maimonides, whose learning and abilities
have been freely acknowledged, both by Jews and Christians. He died in Egypt on the 13th of December, 1204,
having founded a College at Alexandria for the instruction of his countrymen, in which he delivered lectures
on philosophy and the Jewish law.

The **Hot Baths** are about half an hour's walk to the
south of the town; they are supposed to be an infallible
cure for rheumatism, though I had not the courage
to bathe in so filthy a place. The temperature of
the principal spring is 131°-142° Fahrenheit. The **old
castle,** situated on the south side of the town, is interesting for the sake of its view. The **Catholic Convent**
is on the sea-shore, a short distance from the Jews'
Quarter. Here travelers not provided with tents can obtain
accommodation.

The most celebrated Christian tradition is, that the
miraculous draught of fishes took place in the lake, close
by where the Catholic Monastery stands(see above).

Sea of Galilee

The scenery of the Lake of Galilee has been described so often that it needs no description here. It should be seen at sunrise or sunset, when the brown hills are brilliant with color; at eventide, when the shadows deepen in the water; or, best of all, by moonlight, when all that is monotonous in tone is softened, and all inequalities and barrenness are harmonized.

"The lake is pear-shaped, the broad end being towards the north; the greatest width is six and three-quarter miles from Mejdel—'Magdala'—to Khersa—'Gergesa'—about one-third of the way down; and the extreme length is twelve and a quarter miles. The Jordan enters at the north, a swift, muddy stream, coloring the lake a good mile from its mouth, and passes out pure and bright at the south. On the northwestern shore of the lake is a plain, two and a half miles long and one mile broad, called by the Bedouins *El-Ghuweir*, but better known by its familiar name of Gennesareth; and on the northeast, near Jordan's mouth, is a swampy plain, El Batihah, now much frequented by wild boars—formerly the scene of a skirmish between the Jews and Romans, in which Josephus met with an accident that necessitated his removal to Capernaum. * * * On the south, the fine open Valley of the Jordan stretches away towards the Dead Sea, and is covered in the neighborhood of the lake with luxuriant grass."—(Capt. Wilson, "Recovery of Jerusalem.")

The Lake of Galilee is from 600 to 700 feet below the Mediterranean. The water is bright, and good for drinking purposes. It is still subject to violent storms as in the days of the Gospels, and Captain Wilson has well described a storm he witnessed, which singularly well illustrates the Gospel narrative.

Boats on the Lake.—With the greatest interest for the associations of this sacred sea, we had, as the sea was calm, an enjoyable sail upon the lake from Tiberias to Capernaum.

From Tiberias to Tell-Hûm

Almost opposite Tiberias are **Wady Fîk** and the ruins of **Gamala,** where once stood a fortress, garrisoned by Josephus, and taken in A. D. 69 by Vespasian with a loss of ten thousand, half of whom leaped from the walls down the precipices. On the left are some springs, known as **'Ain-el-Bârideh,** then on the left again is seen the village of **Mejdel,** corresponding with **Magdala,** where Mary Magdalene was born. It is a worthless village now, with only twenty huts. Below is a small plain, and with this the traveler will associate the passage in Matt. 15.39, where, after recording the miracle of the loaves and fishes, it is said Jesus "sent away the multitude, and took ship and came into the coast of Magdala." Probably a village named Dalmanutha adjoined Magdala, as in the corresponding passage in Mark 8.10, it says: "Straightway He entered into a ship with His disciples, and came into the parts (? ports) of Dalmanutha."

The level tract beyond Magdala is the **Land of Gennesaret** (Matt. 14.34), now called El Ghuweir, or "the

Little Ghôr." The meaning of the name is supposed to have been either Valley of the Flowers, or Gardens of the Prince. It is about three miles long, and its greatest breadth is one mile. The soil of the whole tract is extremely fruitful, and although the greater part is overrun with rank weeds, the cultivated parts supply the markets of Damascus and Beyrout with the best melons and cucumbers grown in Palestine. It will be remembered that Josephus gives a most glowing description of the Land of Gennesaret, and as the passage occurs so often in the controversy which has been going on for the past few years as to the identity of the site of Capernaum, it will be well to quote it here:

"One may call this place the 'ambition of nature,' when it forces those plants that are naturally enemies to one another, to agree together. It is a happy contention of the seasons, as if every one of them had a claim in this country; for it not only nourishes different sorts of autumnal fruits beyond men's expectations, but preserves them also a great while. It supplies men with the principal fruits—with grapes and figs continually during ten months of the year, and the rest of the fruits as they become ripe together through the whole year; for besides the good temperature of the air, it is also watered from a most fertile fountain. The people of the country call it Capharnaum."—(Josephus iii., ch. 10.8.)

All this region is sacred with associations connected with the ministry of our Lord; and it will be well, perhaps, to quote some of the principal Scripture passages relating to a place so memorable.

Biblical Allusions and Events.—The Sea of Galilee is called in the Old Testament "the Sea of Chinnereth" (Numb. 34.11; Deut. 3.17), and the "Sea of Cinneroth" (Josh. 12.3), from a town which stood somewhere on its margin named Chinnereth (Josh. 19.35). In the New

Testament it is called the "Sea of Tiberias" (John 6.1), from the town of that name; and the "Lake of Gennesareth" (Luke 5.1), from the beautiful plain of Gennesaret. (The modern name is *Bahr Tuberîyeh*.)

In this region, round about the shores of this sea, our Lord spent the principal part of His public life. Nine cities then stood upon its shores, of which the chief were Capernaum, Chorazin, Tiberias, Magdala, and the two Bethsaidas. To tell of all the mighty works performed here would be to transcribe a very considerable part of the four gospels. Every inch, too, is controversial ground, and therefore it will be better merely to give an *epitome* of the scenes which make hill and valley, and shore and sea so intensely sacred.

Cast out from Nazareth, Capernaum (page 194) became henceforth the "home" of Jesus. It was "His own city"; "leaving Nazareth He came and dwelt in Capernaum, which is upon the seacoast, in the borders of Zabulon and Nephthalim: that it might be fulfilled which was spoken by Esaias the prophet, saying, The Land of Zabulon and the land of Nephthalim, by the way of the sea, beyond Jordan, Galilee of the Gentiles; the people which sat in darkness saw great light; and to them which sat in the region and shadow of death light is sprung up" (Matt. 4.13-16). From that time Jesus began to preach, and to say, Repent: for the kingdom of heaven is at hand. Here He called Peter, James, and John, the three most intimate disciples, the "inner circle," of His chosen band. "And it came to pass, that, as the people pressed upon Him to hear the word of God, He stood by the lake of Gennesaret, and saw two ships standing by the lake: but the fishermen were gone out of them, and were washing their nets" (Luke 5.1). Then He entered into Simon's ship, and taught the people on the shore, and after that He performed the miracle of the draught of fishes, which so astonishing Peter, James, and John, the Master said to them, "Fear not; from henceforth thou shalt catch men. And when they had brought their ships to shore, they forsook all, and followed Him."

From a ship on the waters of this lake, He delivered that marvelous discourse on the kingdom of heaven. Jesus "went out of His house ('His own house') and sat by the seaside. And great multitudes were gathered unto Him, so that He went into a ship and sat; and the whole multitude stood on the shore" (Matt. 13.1,2), and heard those wonderful parables of the sower, the wheat and the tares, the grain of mustard-seed, the leaven, and the net cast into the sea.

Here when "there arose a great tempest in the sea, insomuch that the ship was covered with waves * * * He rebuked the winds and the sea, and there was a great calm. But the men marvelled, saying, What manner of man is this, that even the winds and the sea obey Him! And when He was come to the other side into the country of the Gergesenes, there met Him two possessed with devils, coming out of the tombs, exceeding fierce, so that no man might pass by that way. And behold, they cried out, saying, What have we to do with Thee, Jesus, thou Son of God? art Thou come hither to torment us before the time? And there was a good way off from them an herd of many swine feeding. So the devils besought Him saying, If Thou cast us out, suffer us to go away into the herd of swine. And He said unto them, Go. And when they were come out, they went into the herd of swine: and, behold, the whole herd of swine ran violently down a steep place into the sea, and perished in the waters" (Matt. 8.28-34). Near here He fed the five thousand (page 178), and afterwards seeing His disciples toiling in rowing on the lake, for the wind was contrary, "Jesus went unto them, walking on the sea" (Matt. 14.25). "And in the fourth watch of the night Jesus went unto them, walking on the sea. And when the disciples saw Him walking on the sea, they were troubled, saying, It is a spirit; and they cried out for fear. But straightway Jesus spake unto them, saying, Be of good cheer; it is I; be not afraid. And Peter answered Him and said, Lord, if it be Thou, bid me come unto Thee on the water. And He said, Come. And when Peter was come down out of the ship, he walked on the water, to go to Jesus. But when he saw the wind boisterous, he was afraid; and beginning to sink, he cried, saying, Lord, save me. And immediately Jesus stretched forth His hand, and caught him, and said unto him, O thou of little faith, wherefore didst thou doubt?"

When the collectors of tribute came to Him at Capernaum, our Lord, in the exhibition of His perfect and complete humanity, linked Himself with His disciples in one of His most touching utterances. Having elicited from Peter that the tribute should be taken from strangers, and that the children should go free, He added, "Notwithstanding, lest we should offend them, go thou to the sea, and cast a hook, and take up the fish that first cometh up; and when thou hast opened his mouth, thou shalt find a piece of money: that take, *and give unto them for Me and thee*" (Matt. 17.27).

Here He "performed many mighty works" and "spake many things," and here was the scene of those touching incidents which occurred soon after His resurrection. One early morning, the disciples who were in their boat, after having toiled all the night and caught nothing, saw a dim figure standing "on the shore"—probably the beach of the plain of Gennesaret. A voice, strangely familiar, yet unrealized, came to them, "Children, have ye any meat?" And when they replied "No," and the first miracle on their entry to the discipleship was repeated, then "that disciple whom Jesus loved" first, with the

quick instinct of love, said, "It is the Lord;" while Peter,
first with the impetuosity of a love of service, cast himself into the sea, and swam to Him. And there on the
shore, where the mysterious fire of coals burned, and
the farewell meal was spread, the Lord bade them dine.
And there the disciple who, three times warned, had
thrice denied his Lord, by threefold confession was restored and reinstated in the apostolic office (John 21).

These are but scanty specimens. Other events will be
referred to under their proper heads, but the hints suggested in the preceding passages will give the traveler
a clue to many a sacred thought and feeling.

"This is a hallowed lake in the glorious Land of Promise and Divine performance—the peaceful scene of the
opening career of the Redeemer, the cradle of His teaching, the country of His disciples; His chosen retreat
when He hid himself from His foes; His miracles and
His sublime lessons have consecrated these solitudes.
The charm of this landscape is felt still in our own day,
and is reflected in the simple story of the Evangelists.
We are carried back to the life on its shores by the parable of the net, by that of the lost sheep, by the image of
the sheep-fold, and the beautiful lesson of the lilies.
These flowers, more glorious than Solomon's purple,
still abound * * *"—(Ritter Erdkunda.)

And as He taught in Capernaum (Luke 7.36-50), "one
of the Pharisees desired Him that He would eat with
him. And He went into the Pharisee's house, and sat
down to meat. And, behold, a woman in the city, which
was a sinner, when she knew that Jesus sat at meat in the
Pharisee's house, brought an alabaster box of ointment,
and stood at His feet behind Him weeping, and began
to wash His feet with tears, and did wipe *them* with the
hairs of her head, and kissed His feet, and anointed them
with the ointment. Now when the Pharisee which had

bidden Him saw it, he spake within himself, saying, This
man, if He were a prophet, would have known who and
what manner of woman *this is* that toucheth Him: for
she is a sinner. And Jesus answering said unto him,
Simon, I have somewhat to say unto thee. And he saith,
Master, say on.

"There was a certain creditor which had two debtors:
the one owed five hundred pence, and the other fifty.
And when they had nothing to pay, he frankly forgave
them both. Tell Me therefore, which of them will love
him most? Simon answered and said, I suppose that *he,*
to whom he forgave most. And He said unto him, Thou
hast rightly judged. And He turned to the woman, and
said unto Simon, Seest thou this woman? I entered into
thine house, thou gavest Me no water for My feet: but
she hath washed My feet with tears, and wiped *them* with
the hairs of her head. Thou gavest Me no kiss; but the
woman since the time I came in hath not ceased to kiss
My feet. My head with oil thou didst not anoint: but
this woman hath anointed My feet with ointment:
Wherefore I say unto thee, Her sins which are many,
are forgiven; for she loved much: but to whom little is
forgiven, *the same* loveth little. And He said unto her,
Thy sins are forgiven. And they that sat at meat with Him
began to say within themselves, Who is this that for-
giveth sins also? And He said to the woman, Thy
faith hath saved thee; go in peace."

Tell-Hûm

Tell-Hûm is two miles west of the Jordan. It is a mass of ruins, in the early summer overgrown with tall, coarse thistles which hide them from view.

The principal ruins are of those of the "White Synagogue," as it has been called on account of its having been built of white limestone; it was 74 feet 9 inches long, by 56 feet 9 inches wide. Connected with this are the ruins of an older building, supposed to be the remains of a basilica enclosing the house of St. Peter, described by Antoninus A. D. 600. Captain Wilson says of the former of these buildings, "If Tell-Hûm be Capernaum, this is without a doubt the synagogue built by the Roman centurion, and one of the most sacred places on earth." (Luke 7.3,4.5-10.) "And when he heard of Jesus, he sent unto Him the elders of the Jews, beseeching Him that He would come and heal His servant. And when they came to Jesus, they besought Him instantly, saying, That he was worthy for whom He should do this: For he loveth our nation, and he hath built us a synagogue. Then Jesus went with them. And when He was now not far from the house, the centurion sent friends to Him, saying unto Him, Lord, trouble not Thyself: for I am not worthy that Thou shouldest enter under my roof. Wherefore neither thought I myself worthy to come unto Thee: but say in a word, and my servant shall be healed. For I also am a man set under authority,

having under me soldiers, and I say unto one, Go, and
he goeth; and to another, Come, and he cometh; and to
my servant, Do this, and he doeth *it*. When Jesus heard
these things, He marveled at him, and turned Him about,
and said unto the people that followed Him, I say unto
you, I have not found so great faith, no, not in Israel.
And they that were sent, returning to the house, found
the servant whole that had been sick."

It was in this building that our Lord gave the well-
known discourse in John 6, on the Bread of Life, verses
25-71. "And when they had found Him on the other
side of the sea, they said unto Him, Rabbi, when camest
Thou hither? Jesus answered them and said, Verily,
verily, I say unto you, Ye seek Me, not because ye saw
the miracles, but because ye did eat of the loaves, and
were filled. Labour not for the meat which perisheth,
but for that meat which endureth unto everlasting life,
which the Son of Man shall give unto you: for Him hath
God the Father sealed. Then said they unto Him, What
shall we do, that we might work the works of God?
Jesus answered and said unto them, This is the work of
God, that ye believe on Him whom He hath sent. They
said therefore unto Him, What sign shewest Thou then,
that we may see, and believe Thee? what dost Thou work?
Our fathers did eat manna in the desert; as it is written,
He gave them bread from heaven to eat. Then Jesus
said unto them, Verily, verily, I say unto you, Moses
gave you not that bread from heaven; but My Father
giveth you the true bread from heaven. For the bread
of God is He which cometh down from heaven, and giveth life unto the world. Then said they unto Him, Lord,
evermore give us this bread. And Jesus said unto them,
I am the bread of life: he that cometh to Me shall never
hunger; and he that believeth on Me shall never thirst.
But I say unto you, That ye also have seen Me, and

believe not. All that the Father giveth Me shall come
to Me; and him that cometh to Me I will in no wise cast
out. For I came down from heaven, not to do Mine
own will, but the will of Him that sent Me. And this
is the Father's will which hath sent Me, that of all which
He hath given Me, I should lose nothing, but should raise
it up again at the last day. And this is the will of Him
that sent Me, that every one which seeth the Son, and
believeth on Him, may have everlasting life: and I will
raise him up at the last day. The Jews then murmured
at Him, because He said, I am the bread which came down
from heaven. And they said, Is not this Jesus, the son
of Joseph, whose father and mother we know? how is it
then that He saith, I came down from heaven? Jesus
therefore answered and said unto them, Murmur not
among yourselves. No man can come to Me, except the
Father which hath sent Me draw him: and I will raise
him up at the last day. It is written in the prophets,
And they shall be all taught of God. Every man therefore that hath heard, and hath learned of the Father,
cometh unto Me. Not that any man hath seen the
Father, save He which is of God, He hath seen the
Father. Verily, verily, I say unto you, He that believeth
on Me hath everlasting life. I am that bread of life.
Your fathers did eat manna in the wilderness, and are
dead. This is the bread which cometh down from
heaven, that a man may eat thereof, and not die. I am
the living bread which came down from heaven: if any
man eat of this bread, he shall live forever: and the bread
that I will give is My flesh, which I will give for the life
of the world. The Jews therefore strove among themselves, saying, How can this man give us His flesh to
eat? Then Jesus said unto them, Verily, verily, I say
unto you, Except ye eat the flesh of the Son of Man, and
drink His blood, ye have no life in you. Whoso eateth

My flesh, and drinketh My blood, hath eternal life; and
I will raise him up at the last day. For My flesh is meat
indeed, and My blood is drink indeed. He that eateth
My flesh, and drinketh My blood, dwelleth in Me, and
I in him. As the living Father hath sent Me, and I live
by the Father: so he that eateth Me, even he shall live
by Me. This is that bread which came down from
heaven: not as your fathers did eat manna, and are dead:
he that eateth of this bread shall live forever. These
things said He in the synagogue, as He taught in Capernaum. Many therefore of His disciples, when they had
heard *this,* said, This is an hard saying; who can hear it?
When Jesus knew in Himself that His disciples murmured at it, He said unto them, Doth this offend you?
What and if ye shall see the Son of Man ascend up where
He was before? It is the spirit that quickeneth; the flesh
profiteth nothing; the words that I speak unto you, *they*
are spirit, and *they* are life. But there are some of you
that believe not. For Jesus knew from the beginning
who they were that believed not, and who should be-
tray Him. And he said, Therefore said I unto you, that
no man can come unto Me, except it were given unto him
of My Father. From that *time* many of His disciples
went back, and walked no more with Him. Then said
Jesus unto the twelve, Will ye also go away? Then
Simon Peter answered Him, Lord, to whom shall we go?
Thou hast the words of eternal life. And we believe and
are sure that Thou art that Christ, the Son of the living
God. Jesus answered them, Have not I chosen you
twelve, and one of you is a devil. He spake of Judas
Iscariot, *the son* of Simon: for he it was that should be-
tray Him, being one of the twelve."
  " 'These things said He in the synagogue, as He taught
in Capernaum' (John 6.59); and it was not without a
certain strange feeling that on turning over a large block

we found the pot of manna engraved on its face, and remembered the words, 'I am that bread of life. Your fathers did eat manna in the wilderness, and are dead.'"

"And it came to pass, the day after, that He went into a city called **Nain**; and many of His disciples went with Him, and much people. Now when He came nigh to the gate of the city, behold, there was a dead man carried out, the only son of his mother, and she was a widow: and much people of the city was with her. And when the Lord saw her, He had compassion on her, and said unto her, Weep not. And He came and touched the bier: and they that bare *him* stood still. And He said, young man, I say unto thee, Arise. And he that was dead sat up, and began to speak. And He delivered him to his mother. And there came a fear on all: and they glorified God, saying, That a great prophet is risen up among us; and, That God hath visited his people. And this rumor of Him went forth throughout all Judæa, and throughout all the region round about."

"And it came to pass afterward that He went throughout every city and village, preaching and shewing the glad tidings of the Kingdom of God: and the twelve *were* with Him. And certain women, which had been healed of evil spirits and infirmities, Mary called Magdalene, out of whom went seven devils, and Joanna, the wife of Chuza Herod's steward, and Susanna, and many others, which ministered unto Him of their substance."

On rising ground at the back of these ruins (those of the "White Synagogue") are the remains of the ancient town of Capernaum, where our Lord had His own house. These ruins occupy a space half a mile long by a quarter of a mile broad. It has been supposed that a main street can be traced, leading to Chorazin.

It is pleasant for the traveler who has been wearied with the holy places in all kinds of improbable grottoes and churches, to feel that here he can, without interruption or annoyance, tread in the very footprints of the Master.

All travelers have expressed themselves rapturously about this, and certainly there is no place where moonlight effects can be witnessed with greater pleasure.

"Never will the night that closed that delightful day in the environs of 'His own city' be forgotten by me," says a recent writer. "It was brilliantly moonlight. and standing upon the cliff above our camping-place, the white houses of Tiberias were distinctly visible; the waters of the lake lay calm and placid as when He said, 'Peace, be still, and there was a great calm'; around us were the 'desert places' and the 'mountain tops' which had been the scene of His resting and His prayers. Capernaum, Bethsaida, Chorazin—mounds of rubbish, tangles of thistles, heaps of ruins—these have been cast down, and have passed away; but the 'mighty works' remain, still powerful in blessing; and the 'gracious words' are as fresh, as beautiful, and as life-giving to-day as when He uttered them."

No traveler will leave these memorable sites without recalling those touching words of our Lord:

"Then began He to upbraid the cities wherein most of His mighty works were done, because they repented not: Woe unto thee, Chorazin! Woe unto thee, Bethsaida! for if the mighty works, which were done in you, had been done in Tyre and Sidon, they would have repented long ago in sackcloth and ashes. But I say unto you, It shall be more tolerable for Tyre and Sidon at the day of judgment than for you. And thou, Capernaum, which art exalted unto heaven, shall be brought down to hell: for if the mighty works, which have been

done in thee, had been in Sodom, it would have remained until this day. But I say unto you, That it shall
be more tolerable for the land of Sodom in the day of judgment, than for thee."—(Matt. 11.20-24).

Tiberias to Bâniâs

From Tiberias to Capernaum (page 190).

Leaving 'Ain-et-Tin, or Tell-Hûm, we proceed by a
wretchedly bad road, which, nevertheless, was the old
caravan road between Egypt and Damascus, until we
reach a point where, looking back, we take our farewell
peeps at the Lake of Gennesaret and its neighborhood,
and looking forward see the unfolding glories of Hermon and Lebanon. We pass the **Khân Yubb Yûsef,** or
Khân of Joseph's Well, the traditional well into which
the hero of the Bible story was thrown by his brethren;
the Khân is modern and filthily dirty.

On our way here we saw the **Jewish farms,** in the
colony of Rothschild, which he had built just a few years
ago. The town was built by Rothschild for the poor
Jews from Russia, to make their home there and farm.
The houses are all about the same height, and built of
red brick. Near this town were seen the Jews with long
beards and their long curls hanging down on either side
of the face, and with their long coats, going behind the
plows and cultivating the land. All things grow splen-
didly here, as the soil is very rich.

While here, we may also read up the following par-
ticulars about the **district of Hûleh,** in which 'Ain Mel-
lâhah is situated. In the Old Testament the **Lake of
Hûleh**—a triangular body of water four and a half miles

long, three and a half broad, eleven feet deep, and nearly
three hundred feet above the sea level—is called **Waters
of Merom.** It was here that Jabin, King of Hazor, gathered together all the surrounding kings and their companies, "and they went out, they and all their hosts with
them, much people, even as the sand that is upon the
seashore in multitude, with horses and chariots very
many. And when all these kings were met together, they
came and pitched together at the waters of Merom, to
fight against Israel. And the Lord said unto Joshua,
Be not afraid because of them : for to-morrow about this
time will I deliver them up all slain before Israel : thou
shalt hough their horses, and burn their chariots with
fire. So Joshua came, and all the people of war with
him, against them by the waters of Merom suddenly ;
and they fell upon them. And the Lord delivered them
into the hand of Israel" (Joshua 11.4-8).

A journey of about an hour from 'Ain Belât across the
plain brings us to a spot of great interest—it is **Tell-el-
Kâdi** (the Hill of the Judge, or the Judge's Mound) corresponding with the **Dan** of Scripture and the Laish of
the Phœnicians. The Tell, or mound, is about a quarter of a mile in diameter, and about fifty feet above the
plain ; beneath it bursts out a beautiful crystal spring,
which sends forth its living stream through the plain ;
while from beneath a wide-spreading terebinth—which
marks the site of a Moslem grave on the side of the
mound—issue some sparkling rills, which add their contributions to the stream. The mound, with the further
mound rising behind it, marks the site of the town and
citadel of Dan, the northern frontier of the Holy Land ;
while the spring at its foot is the **Fountain of the Jordan,**
one of the largest and most important springs of that
sacred river. The history of Dan is briefly as follows :
When Abraham pursued the captors of Lot, he "went

even unto Dan," and with the few men of his household
recovered him and the booty. It was the most northerly
city of Palestine, as Beersheba was the most southerly;
and the expression, "from Dan to Beersheba," is known
to all, both in its literal and metaphorical sense. It was
used in the same way ages ago (see Judges 20.1; 1 Sam.
3.20, etc.).

The journey from Tell-el-Kâdi, or Dan, to Bâniâs, is
short, but exceedingly beautiful, and has been thus ad-
mirably described by Stanley:

"With Dan, the Holy Land properly terminated. But
the easternmost source of the Jordan, about four miles
distant, is so intimately connected with it, both by historical and geographical association, that we must go
forwards yet a little way into the bosom of Hermon.
Over an unshaded carpet of turf—through trees of every
variety of foliage—through a park-like verdure, which
casts a strangely beautiful interest over this last recess
of Palestine, the pathway winds, and the snowy top of
the mountain itself is gradually shut out from view by
its increasing nearness; and again there is a rush of
waters through deep thickets, and the ruins of an ancient
town—not Canaanite, but Roman—rise on the hillside;
in its situation, in its exuberance of water, its olive
groves, and its views over the distant plain, almost a
Syrian Tivoli."

Bâniâs or Cæsarea Philippi

[The usual camping-place is beside the stream flowing
from the source of the Jordan. It is a picturesque spot,
in a fine grove of olives, and green park-like grass, com-

manding too some charming peeps across the ravine.]

Bâniâs was known as the Greek Paneas, from the sanctuary of Pan. It was adorned by Herod the Great, who erected a temple over the spring of the Jordan, in honor of Augustus Cæsar. His son, Philip the Tetrarch, enlarged the town, and called it Cæsarea, in honor of Tiberias Cæsar, and, as there was already a Cæsarea on the Mediterranean, he added Philippi. By Agrippa II. it was named Neronias, but this name soon died out, and it became generally known as Cæsarea Paneas, a name which is preserved in the modern name of Bâniâs.

Nothing is known of the very ancient history of this remarkable place, although Drs. Robinson and Schwarz agree that it corresponds with Baal-Gad, the northern boundary of Joshua's victories. "Joshua took the land, even from the Mount of Halak that goeth up to Seir, even unto Baal-Gad in the valley of Lebanon under Mount Hermon" (Joshua 11.17, see also 12.7,13.5).

Baal-Gad is probably identical with Baal-Hermon (Judges 3.3; 1 Chron. 5.23).

The situation of Bâniâs is exceptionally beautiful, being on the mountain slope, with ravines on either side. and everywhere sparkling streams of water and therefore luxuriant vegetation. The modern village has about fifty or sixty houses, and one or two shops. There is a rough bridge over the Jordan made of antique pillars minus the capitals; parts of the old citadel are still to be seen, and its massive walls and towers can be traced.

Several picturesque views may be obtained among the ruins, especially from the bridge and the citadel. These will not attract the interest of the visitor, who will at once proceed to the spot where all the present interest in Bâniâs centers. It is the fountain or Source of the Jordan, which bursts out in a series of many streams, and, forming a large basin, flows hence in one copious stream. Behind it rises a precipitous red lime-stone cliff, in the face of which is a **cave**, or **grotto**, the Paneum, or **Sanctuary of Pan**, from which the town took its name. On the summit of the cliff Herod erected a white marble temple; now there is a *wely* in honour of St. George on the same spot.

As we stand at the foot of the cave and look at that grotto, where, perchance, in early days Baal was wor-shipped, where, without doubt, the Greeks, who always associated caves and grottoes with the worship of Pan, paid their devotions to that deity, we recall with some emotion that scene recorded in Matt. 16.13, "When Jesus came into the coasts of Cæsarea Philippi: He asked His disciples, saying, Whom do men say that I, the Son of Man am? And they said, Some say that Thou art the John the Baptist; some, Elias; and others, Jeremias, or one of the prophets. He saith unto them, But whom say ye that I am? And Simon Peter answered and said, Thou art the Christ, the Son of the living God. And Jesus answered and said unto him, Blessed art thou, Simon Bar-jona: for flesh and blood hath not revealed it unto thee, but my Father which is in heaven. And I say also unto thee, That thou art Peter, and upon this rock I will build My church; and the gates of hell shall not prevail against it."

Mount Hermon

Hermon ("Lofty or Prominent Peak") occupies a most commanding position, and is visible from Sarepta, Tyre, and even from the depths of the Jordan valley by the

Dead Sea. Its ancient names all describe this position.
Sion (Deut. 4.48) ("the Upraised"), so named because
it towers above the other mountains. Sirion ("the Glittering") it was called by the Sidonians; Shenir ("the
Clattering") by the Amorites (Deut. 3.9). Both of these
words, too, mean "Breastplate." The mountain is now
called Jebel-esh-Shiekh ("the Chief Mountain")—also
suggestive of its imposing appearance. Twice in Scripture the name of Baal-Hermon is given to the mountain
—no doubt the result of the worship of Baal in that
"high place" (Judges 3.3; 1 Chron. 5.23).

Mount Hermon has been called Mont Blanc of Palestine. It was the great landmark for the northern border of the Israelites, and it rises about ten thousand
feet above the level of the sea. There are three separate heights which form the summit, and they rise two
or three thousand feet above the main chain. The views
from the summit are, of course, very extensive and
deeply interesting. That from the greatest height takes
in Bukâ'a, and the ranges of Lebanon and Anti-Lebanon.
The great eastern plain is well stretched out before the
second or southern height; and from the third or western peak a great part of Syria is seen. Far away to the
south are the mountains of 'Ajlûn, stretching towards
Moab; and we can follow with the eye the course of the
Jordan, with the lakes of Tiberias and Hûleh, the mountains of Gilead on the one side, and those of Samaria on
the other. On the west lie Samaria and Galilee, reaching to Carmel, which is seen, together with Tyre and
the Mediterranean. Beyond Tyre rises the range of Lebanon, which prevents our seeing further north. We see
Anti-Libanus and the Plain of Damascus, which extend
as far as the "Meadow Lakes" in the northwest. To the
south of this limit rise conspicuously to view the complete chain of the Haurân.

Hermon is the second mountain of Syria for height, being perhaps only three or four hundred feet lower than the highest point of Lebanon. Limestone composes the main part of the mountain. The loftiest peak, which is an obtuse truncated cone, is quite destitute of trees and verdure, and the snow never disappears from its summit. In spring and summer it is thickly covered, but as the year advances it partially melts, and has a streaked appearance, and at last only a few white lines, until the winter again, early in November, gives it the great white dome. A ravine on the north side divides Hermon from Anti-Libanus. Bears (*Ursus Syriacus*) are to be found on Mount Hermon, very much like the brown bear. Game abounds, too, and foxes and wolves are found on the slopes.

April is the month when the blossoms abound. The vine on Mount Hermon is cultivated on its slopes, and several wild fruits are found high up; and on the western slope, at no less a height than over five thousand feet, the almond-tree flourishes to such an extent that this part has received the name *Akabet el Lozi* (Almond Mountain). Vegetation gradually ceases towards the top, and near the snowy crown nothing but the *Ranunculus Demisus* is found.—(L. H.)

From Bâniâs to Damascus

Almost immediately after leaving Bâniâs the ascent commences, and the roads are bad. We passed a Druse village, **Mejdel,** and then a series of further ascents were made, while the head of Hermon, which is covered deeply with snow, as late as to the end of May, lay on our left.

A lofty plain, named **Merj-el-Hadr,** was crossed, and a wild glen with a noisy stream entered; then down, sometimes past oases of beauty in wildernesses of desolation, until a halt was made in a rocky valley near **Beit Jenn.** A pleasant road travels beside the brook, called at this part Jenâni. After about forty minutes' ride, we enter a large plain, with remarkably fine views all round, and especially of Hermon, but no place of importance is visited until Kefr-Hawar is reached.

Kefr-Hawar is the usual camping-place between Bâniâs and Damascus; the village is large, and surrounded by pleasant gardens and groves; the houses are curiously built, terrace upon terrace, on the hillside. The inhabitants are Moslems, and are not always very friendly to Christian travelers who encamp outside their village; care should be taken, therefore, not to give any occasion of offence. There is nothing in the village to call for special attention, except an unknown ruin, and a tradition as to its being the burial-place of Nimrod.

Proceeding towards Damascus, whether we go by the road to the right or that to the left, we have before us a long, wearisome ride over a bleak desert, without anything to attract special attention, until we reach a spot where the old Roman road, leading to Damascus from Egypt and Palestine is gained. It is a spot which will be forever memorable, as there is no good reason to doubt the tradition which states that here St. Paul beheld the wondrous vision which attended his conversion "As he journeyed, he came near Damascus: and suddenly there shined round about him a light from heaven: and he fell to the earth, and heard a voice saying unto him, Saul, Saul, why persecutest thou Me? * * * And he trembling and astonished said, Lord, what wilt Thou have me to do? And the Lord said unto him, Arise, and go into the city, and it shall be told thee what thou must do * * * And Saul arose from the earth; and when his eyes were opened, he saw no man; but they led him by the hand, and brought him into Damascus. And he was three days without sight, and neither did eat nor drink. And there was a certain disciple at Damascus, named Ananias; and to him said the Lord in a vision, Ananias. And he said, Behold, I *am here* Lord. And the Lord said unto him, Arise, and go into the street which is called Straight, and enquire in the house of Judas for *one* called Saul, of Tarsus: for, behold, he prayeth, and hath seen in a vision a man named Ananias coming in, and putting *his* hand on him, that he might receive his sight. Then Ananias answered, Lord, I have heard by many of this man, how much evil he hath done to Thy saints at Jerusalem: And here he hath authority from the chief priests to bind all that call on Thy name But the Lord said unto him, Go thy way: for he is a chosen vessel unto Me, to bear My name before the Gentiles, and kings, and the children of Israel: For I will shew him how great things he must suffer for My name's sake. And Ananias went his way, and entered into the house; and putting his hands on him said, Brother Saul, the Lord, *even* Jesus, that appeared unto thee in the way as thou camest, hath sent me, that thou mightest receive thy sight, and be filled with the Holy Ghost. And immediately there fell from his eyes as it had been scales: and he received sight forthwith, and arose, and was baptized. Then was Saul certain days with the disciples which were at Damascus. And straightway he preached Christ in the synagogues, that He is the Son of God. But all that heard *him* were amazed, and said: Is not this he that destroyed them which called on this name—in Jerusalem, and came hither for that intent, that he might bring them bound unto the chief priests? But Saul increased the more in strength, and con-

founded the Jews which dwelt at Damascus, proving that
this is very Christ. And after that many days were fulfilled, the Jews took counsel to kill him: But their laying await was known of Saul, and they watched the
gates day and night to kill him. Then the disciples took
him by night, and let *him* down by the wall in a basket.
And when Saul was come to Jerusalem, he assayed to
join himself to the disciples: but they were all afraid
of him, and believed not that he was a disciple. But
Barnabas took him, and brought *him* to the Apostles,
and declared unto them how he had seen the Lord in
the way, and that he had spoken to him, and how he
had preached boldly at Damascus in the name of Jesus.
And he was with them coming in and going out at Jerusalem. And he spake boldly in the name of the Lord
Jesus, and disputed against the Grecians: but they went
about to slay him. Which when the brethren knew,
they brought him down to Cæsarea, and sent him forth
to Tarsus" (Acts 9).

Before us lay the great plain of Damascus, a sea of
verdure; in the distance, to the right, I saw the white
minarets of the city, on the left the magnificent slopes
of Lebanon; around, streams of water. Several towns
and villages, without anything remarkable about them
to call for special notice, were passed, and then the groves
and gardens for which Damascus is so famous were entered, and the waters of Abana and Pharpar, which seem
"to be better than all the waters of Israel," were beside
us, and we entered the gate of the oldest city in the world.

Damascus

[Travelers in Damascus who wish to wander about in the city after dark must be careful to carry a lantern; if found without one, they will find themselves under arrest, and find the position unpleasant into the bargain. These lanterns are simple contrivances, not unlike the Chinese lanterns used for Christmas trees. If the traveler finds his progress after dusk interrupted by a closed gate, he must shout, *"Ifta ya Hâris!" i. e.,* "Open, O watchman," and give a trifling fee. Here, as elsewhere, a fee will cover almost every difficulty.]

Damascus is the oldest city in the world. (Josephus makes it even older than Abraham—Ant. 1.63). For the traditions of the events in the infancy of the human race, which are supposed to have happened in its vicinity, see Pococke 2.115,116. Abraham's steward was "Eliezer of Damascus" (Gen. 15.2).

Its fame begins with the earliest patriarchs, and continues to modern times. While other cities of the East have risen and decayed, Damascus is still what it was.

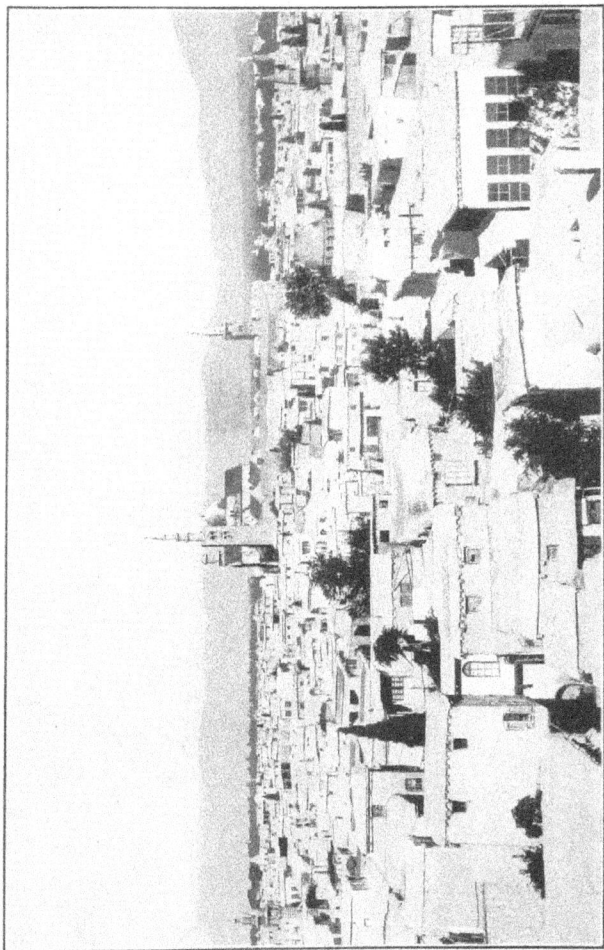

DAMASCUS.

It was founded before Ba'albek and Palmyra, and it has outlived them both. While Babylon is a heap in the desert, and Tyre a ruin on the shore, it remains what it is called in the Prophecies of Isaiah—"the head of Syria" (Isaiah 7.8).

How important a place it was in the flourishing period of the Jewish monarchy, we know from the garrisons which David placed there (2 Sam. 8.6; 1 Chron. 18.6), and from the opposition it presented to Solomon (1 Kings 11.24). The history of Naaman and the Hebrew captive, Elisha and Gehazi, and of the proud preference of its fresh rivers to the thirsty waters of Israel, are familiar to every one. And how close its relations continued to be with the Jews we know from the chronicles of Jeroboam and Ahaz, and the prophecies of Isaiah and Amos (see 2 Kings 14.28,16.9,10; 2 Chron. 24.23,28.5-23; Isaiah 7.8; Amos 1.3-5).

Its mercantile greatness is indicated by Ezekiel in the remarkable words addressed to Tyre. (The port of Beyrout is now to Damascus what Tyre was of old.) "Syria was thy merchant by reason of the multitude of the wares of thy making; they occupied in thy fairs with emeralds, purple, and broidered work, and fine linen, and coral, and agate. Damascus was thy merchant in the multitude of the wares of thy making, for the multitude of all riches; in the wine of Helbon, and white wool" (Ezek. 27.16,18). Leaving the Jewish annals, we might follow its history through continuous centuries, from the time when Alexander sent Parmenio to take it, while the conqueror himself was marching from Tarsus to Tyre— (*Quintus Curtius* 3.13; 4.1; Arrian 2.11)—to its occupation by Pompey. Its relative importance was not so great when it was under a Western power, like that of the Seleucids or the Romans; hence we find it less frequently mentioned than we might expect by Greek and

Roman writers. This arose from the building of Antioch, and other cities in Northern Syria—to the letters of Julian the Apostate, who describes it as "the eye of the East"—and onward through the golden days when it was the residence of the Ommiad Caliphs, and the metropolis of the Mohammedan world—and through the period when its fame was mingled with that of Saladin and Tamerlane—to our own days, when the praise of its beauty is celebrated by every traveler from Europe. It is evident, to use the words of Lamartine, that, like Constantinople, it was a "predestinated capital." Nor is it difficult to explain why its freshness has never faded through all this series of vicissitudes and wars.

Among the rocks and brushwood at the base of Anti-Libanus are the fountains of a copious and perennial stream, which, after running a course of no great distance to the southeast, loses itself in a desert lake. But before it reaches this dreary boundary, it has distributed its channels over the intermediate space, and left a wide area behind it, rich with prolific vegetation. These are the "streams from Lebanon," which are known to us in the imagery of Scripture (Song of Sol. 4.15), and the "rivers of Damascus," which Naaman, not unnaturally, preferred to all the "waters of Israel."

By Greek writers, the stream is called Chrysorrhoas (Strabo 16.2; Ptolem. 5.15-19. See Pliny N. H. 5.16), or "the river of gold." And this stream is the inestimable inexhausted treasure of Damascus. "The habitations of men must always have been gathered round it, as the Nile has inevitably attracted an immemorial population to its banks. The desert is a fortification round Damascus. The river is its life. It is drawn out into water courses, and spread in all directions. For miles around it is a wilderness of gardens—gardens with roses among the tangled shrubberies, and with fruit on the branches overhead. Everywhere among the trees the murmur of unseen rivulets is heard. Even in the city, which is in the midst of the garden, the clear rushing of the current is a perpetual refreshment. Every dwelling has its fountain, and at night, when the sun has set behind Mount Lebanon, the lights of the city are seen flashing on the waters."—(Conybeare and Howson's "Life and Epistles of St. Paul.")

Damascus remains the true type of an Oriental city. Caravans come and go from Bagdad and Mecca, as of old; merchants sit and smoke over their costly bales in dim bazaars; drowsy groups sip their coffee in kiosks overhanging the river; and all the picturesque costumes of the East mingle in the streets. The **first view** of the town from one of the overhanging ridges is like a vision of the earthly paradise. Marble minarets, domes glittering with the crescent, massive towers, and terraces of level roofs rise out of a sea of foliage, the white buildings, shining with ivory softness through the broad dark clumps of verdure, which, miles in depth and leagues in circuit, girdle the city—making it, as the people love to say, a pearl set in emeralds. It is a wilderness of bloom, and fragrance, and fruitage, where olive and pomegranate, orange and apricot, plum and walnut, mingle their varied tints of green—a maze of flowering and scented thickets, pierced with wild wood and glades, that are sweet with roses and jasmine blossom, and alive with babbling springs and rivulets. And close up to the forest edge comes the yellow desert, and around it are the bare mountains, with the snowy crest of Hermon, standing like a sentinel with shining helmet, on the west—"the tower of Lebanon which looketh toward Damascus."

The **Biblical Allusions** to Damascus are very numerous. After the reference to it in the time of Abraham

(Gen. 14.15), the next reliable notice is found in 2 Sam.
8.5. "When the Syrians of Damascus came to succour
Hadadezer, king of Zobah, David slew of the Syrians
two and twenty thousand men. Then David put garrisons in Syria of Damascus, and the Syrians became servants to David." For an account of the battles between
the kings of Judah and Israel, and the kings of Damascus, see 1 Chron. 18.5,6; 2 Kings 6, 7, 8, 11, 13, 14, 15,
16. The prophetical utterances concerning the city are
chiefly Isa. 17.; Amos 1.3-5; Jer. 49.23-27. In the new
Testament, it will be remembered that St. Paul was
converted on his way hither (page 203), and that when
"the governor under Aretas the king, kept the city of the
Damascenes with a garrison" (2 Cor. 11.32,33), sought
to apprehend Paul, he was let down in a basket through
a window and escaped his hands. There is no doubt
that there were many synagogues here, for St. Paul,
when he went unto the High Priest, "desired of him
letters to Damascus to the synagogues" (Acts 9.1,2).
During the residence of St. Paul here "he preached Christ
in the synagogues that He is the Son of God * * * and
confounded the Jews which dwelt at Damascus, proving
that this is very Christ" (Acts 9.20-22). Christianity
flourished here so extensively that, in the time of Constantine, the Great Temple was converted into a Christian
church (page 215).

The **population** of Damascus has been variously estimated. In round numbers it may be taken as about two
hundred and fifty thousand, of whom about two hundred
thousand are Moslems, six thousand Jews, thirty thousand Greeks, and Syrians, Maronites three thousand, and
one thousand Armenians, Catholics and Protestants.
They all speak the same language, Arabic, through Syria
as well as in Palestine. The Mohommedans of Damascus are notorious for their fanaticism; and the horrible

massacre of July, 1860, when they fell upon the Christians and slaughtered six thousand of them in the streets, and burned the quarter of the city they inhabited (page 221) is still fresh in memory.

At least several days should be devoted by every traveler to this remarkable city.

The Bazaars

of Damascus are celebrated all the world over, and interested us as long as we stayed in the city; for here, every day, and at all hours of the day, we saw an assemblage of people such as probably cannot be seen in any other bazaar in the East. Although Cairo contains a much larger population than Damascus, its bazaars are by no means so extensive or imposing; nor is it difficult to find the reason of this superiority, for whereas the capital of Egypt supplies chiefly its own inhabitants only, the whole population of the Haurân, as well as the Bedawin of the eastern district, depend upon Damascus for the necessaries and comforts of life.

The bazaars are in long avenues, roofed over; not a mere jumble of miscellaneous shops, but each bazaar devoted to some special trade of manufacture. There is the **Saddlers' Bazaar,** where the gay but uncomfortable Syrian saddles we saw in all their varieties, and any useful articles connected with saddlery, may be purchased. The **Silk Bazaar**—where English travelers generally linger to inspect the gorgeous robes of Damascus work, and to purchase at least one of those gay head-dresses, (*Keffiyeh*) which have charmed them so often in Palestine—is very attractive. There are a variety of specialities to be obtained here, such as worked tablecloths; the *Bedawin 'Abayeh,* or bernouse; silk scarfs, and elegant tobacco pouches. The **Old Clo' Bazaar,** where second-hand clothes and other articles are sold by a mock auction, is a center of attraction, and there is generally a great deal of amusement to be made out of a visit. The **Fez Bazaar** was visited; it revealed all the arts and mysteries of turbans, caps worn under the fez, and the paraphernalia of Oriental head-gear. The **Greek Bazaar** is one of the most attractive, as here antiquities of all kinds are sold, and "Damascus blades" may be bought to the usual disadvantage. Some are really exceedingly pretty, the handles being wrought with all kinds of cunning workmanship. The "coffee sets" sold here are very choice; the cups are so small that five or six of them would only fill an ordinary English coffee-cup. These little vessels are beautifully painted or set in stones, and are fitted into delicately carved, thin, metallic receivers for handing to guests.

In addition to these there is the **Tobacco Bazaar,** where pipes, mouth-pieces, and such like things, can be obtained; the **Booksellers' Bazaar,** where none but Mohammedan books are sold; the **Coppersmith's Bazaar,** where, if the traveler can endure the noise, he will behold some wonderful dishes and culinary utensils; the **Boot and Shoe Bazaar,** where, as in Constantinople, richly decorated slippers and shoes can be obtained, and the yellow leather slippers, which ladies are fond of possessing on account of their softness. Without minutely describing the different bazaars in detail, it may be said that there are bazaars for every branch of trade and manufacture, and we found we could purchase anything from a shoe latchet to a camel.

On Friday, the Market Day, the crowds are enormous, and then the "eye of the East" both sees and is to be seen, to the best advantage. Then, as in fact on other days, there will be seen Persians in gorgeous silks, Nubians in black and white, Greeks in national costume, Jews with ringlets and without, Bedawîn of the desert, pilgrims *en route* to Mecca—a marvelous medley, not to be seen anywhere else. The hubbub is generally terrific. "Now way must be made for some grandee; now a string of camels drives the crowd into a mass, or a party of midshipmen just arrived from Beyrout rush through the bazaars on fleet donkeys, scattering sherbet stalls as they pass. And in the midst of it all, the richly-robed merchants sit in the sills of their shops, smoking their tchibouks and sipping coffee with the most consummate indifference." In addition to the bazaars, we were greatly interested in visiting the **Khâns,** where wholesale trade is carried on. They are for the most part owned by merchants of immense wealth, and the carpets of Persia, the muslins of India, the prints of Manchester, etc., etc., form the stock-in-trade.

The **Shops** are not less curious than bazaars or Khâns; some are devoted to water-coolers and earthenware, some, and these are specially worth visiting, for attar of roses. In the shops devoted to articles of consumption many peculiarities were noticed; bakers' shops filled with thin, warm, flat bread, and cakes; the confectioners', with every variety of colored sweetmeat and pleasant beverages, supposed to be iced with snow from Lebanon; the butchers' shops, though less tempting, were curious from the way in which the meat was cut up, and exposed for sale.

The **street vendors** go about in legions; lemonade, raisin water, fruits, pistachio nuts—in short, everything

that can be hawked about is sold in the streets; the cries
of the sellers are amusing, and, when interpreted, to a
certain extent instructive. The bread boy cries, "O
Allah! who sustainest us, send trade!" the drink seller
cries, "O cheer thine heart!" as he rattles his copper cups
in his hand; and so on.

The Great Mosque

[Until within a few years past, the Great Mosque was
closed to all save Moslems. Now, Christians can obtain
admission; only twenty persons, however, are allowed
at one time, and this only upon application to the Consul.
The charge is four dollars for the party. Slippers, which
are by the door-way, have to be put on before entering
the Mosque.]

The Mosque stands in the midst of a spacious quad-
rangle, and is as large, or larger, than the Mosque of
Omar. It has been pointed out by good authorities that
this building, so venerated by the followers of the
prophet, exhibits three distinct styles of architecture,
marking three great epochs in its history, and proclaim-
ing the three great dynasties that had successively possessed it. First of all it had been a heathen temple, and
its massive stones, and beautiful arches and gate, proclaim Grecian or Roman architecture. Whether the
temple was built by the Seleucidæ, the successors of
Alexander the Great, who reigned in Damascus about a
century before the Christian era, or by the Romans, who
entered it under the leadership of Pompey, B. C. 64, cannot be determined, for these rulers succeeded so closely
upon one another, that no great difference can be discov-

ered, or could be expected, between their respective styles
of architecture. It cannot be questioned, however, that
a heathen temple once stood on this spot, in which for
several centuries, sacrifices were offered to the gods of
Pagan mythology. When the decaying Roman Empire
was divided into two great rival dominions of west and
east, and the power on the banks of the Tiber was out-
shone by the power on the shores of the Bosphorus,
Damascus owned the sway of the Greek Empire at Constantinople, and, after Constantine had embraced Christianity, the temple, which had been sacred to Jupiter, became sacred to Jesus, and was dedicated to John the Baptist. We know that the Christian faith immediately
after the apostolic age advanced rapidly in Damascus;
for church history informs us that, at the Council of Nice,
A. D. 325, convened to pronounce an authoritative opinion on the question of the Divinity of Christ, as raised
by the Arian controversy, its metropolitan bishop attended with seven of his suffragans. Only about fifty
years ago, a Greek inscription was found on a large stone,
at one of the gates, to the following effect: "This Church
of the blessed John Baptist was restored by Arcadius,
the son of Theodosius." Arcadius ascended the throne
A. D. 395, seventy years after the establishment of Christianity by Constantine. His father is well known to have
exerted all his power to extirpate heathen worship from
every part of the empire. During his reign the temple at
Damascus may have been pillaged and partly ruined.
His son restored it, dedicated it to the worship of the
true God, and caused a noble inscription to be placed
above the principal door. There it still stands, as if in
defiance of the crescent that has usurped the place of the
cross, and as if prophetic of the day when Jesus shall
reign over the hearts of the Damascenes:

"Thy kingdom, O Christ, is a kingdom of all ages

[that is, an everlasting kingdom], and thy dominion lasts throughout all generations."

Strange that Moslem fanaticism should have allowed such an inscription to remain upon the chief gate of their consecrated mosque, which sounds so like a protestation against their usurpation of the place.

For nearly three centuries the building continued to be the cathedral church for Syria, while Christianity was predominant in the land. When at last the city fell into the hands of the Moslems, partly by treaty and partly by treachery (A. D. 634), the church was equally divided between the followers of Christ and the followers of the prophet. "On the accession of Walid, the sixth khalif of the Omenyades (A. D. 705), the whole church was demanded by the Moslems. The Christians refused, and showed that, by the terms of the original treaty, their rights were solemnly guaranteed to them. But Moslem policy, then as crooked as it is now, found an easy mode of evading inconvenient treaties; and the poor Christians were compelled to give in. The khalif immediately entered the church with guards, and ordered them to remove or destroy every vestige of Christian worship. Standing on the great altar, Walid himself directed the work of spoliation. Seeing his position, one of his followers, more superstitious or more timid than the rest, thus addressed him: 'Prince of the Faithful, I tremble for your safety. The power of that image against which you stand may be exerted against you.' 'Fear not for me,' replied the proud Moslem, 'for the first spot on which I shall lay my battleaxe will be that image's head.' Thus saying, he lifted his weapon and dashed the image to pieces. The Christians raised a cry of horror, but their voices were drowned in the triumphant shout, 'Ullahu Ak-bar.' Having thus obtained possession, Walid spared neither time nor expense in decorating the building. He

made it the most magnificent mosque in his wide dominions. And even now, neglected and shattered as it is, it
has few equals in the Mohammedan empire."—*Fergusson's
"Sacred and Continental Scenes."*)

There are many things to see in the Mosque and
Haram. The entrance *archway* on the west is antique
and of very beautiful workmanship. The **interior** of the
mosque is impressive, with nave and aisles supported by
columns. The first things to claim attention will be the
number of lamps hung from the ceiling, and the inscriptions from the Koran; the stained windows, the various
praying places, and the handsome carpets covering the
marble pavement. In the transept is a "chapel" said to
contain the **Head of John the Baptist,** also said to have
been found in the crypt of the church.

The **Pulpit** is solid and handsome; the **Mosaics** on the
walls are old.

The **Court** is spacious, and contains in the center a
marble fountain, where the worshippers perform their
ablutions before entering the mosque. Corridors surround the court, and I saw the traces of the gilding with
which they were once beautied. In the western part
of the court is the "Dome of Treasures," containing relics
and MSS. of immense value, but its contents are never
under any circumstances exhibited.

There are **three minarets** to the mosque, and it is usual
to ascend one at least. The **Minaret of the Bride,** is the
most ancient, and commands the best view. It is ascended by 160 steps. The **view** is magnificent. When I
looked down upon the gardens of Damascus, a perfect
fairy land, I saw the silver threads of Barada running
like a network through the city and plain, and gazed
upon the wonderful city crowded with a dense population, with here a cluster of mud huts, side by side with
gaily painted dwellings, with marble courts and foun-

tains, and every appearance of Oriental magnificence;
and all around the bristling minarets of mosques, and the
chief buildings and places of interest. The **Minaret of
Jesus** is so named from a legend that when Jesus comes
to judge the world He will descend first to this minaret.

This mosque may, and, tradition affirms, does, speak
of a very ancient worship; and it is highly probable that
this was the site of the Temple of Rimmon, the god
worshipped by the Syrians. If so, it was here that Naaman deposited his "two mules' burden of earth," and
reared his own altar.

In the story recorded in 2 Kings 5. "Now Naaman,
captain of the host of the king of Syria, was a great man
with his master, and honorable, because by him the Lord
had given deliverance unto Syria: he was also a mighty
man in valor, *but he was* a leper. And the Syrians had
gone out by companies, and had brought away captive
out of the land of Israel a little maid; and she waited
on Naaman's wife. And she said unto her mistress,
Would God my lord *were* with the prophet that *is* in
Samaria! for he would recover him of his leprosy. And
one went in, and told his lord, saying, thus and thus
said the maid that *is* of the land of Israel. And the king
of Syria said, Go to, go, and I will send a letter unto the
king of Israel. And he departed, and took with him ten
talents of silver, and six thousand *pieces* of gold, and ten
changes of raiment. And he brought the letter to the
king of Israel, saying, Now when this letter is come
unto thee, behold, I have *therewith* sent Naaman my
servant to thee, that thou mayest recover him of his
leprosy. And it came to pass, when the king of Israel
had read the letter, that he rent his clothes, and said, Am
I God, to kill and to make alive, that this man doth send
unto me to recover a man of his leprosy? wherefore consider, I pray you, and see how he seeketh a quarrel against

me. And it was *so,* when Elisha the man of God hath heard
that the king of Israel had rent his clothes, that he sent
to the king, saying, Wherefore hast thou rent thy clothes?
let him come now to me, and he shall know that there
is a prophet in Israel. So Naaman came with his horses
and with his chariot, and stood at the door of the house
of Elisha. And Elisha sent a messenger unto him, saying, Go and wash in Jordan seven times, and thy flesh
shall come again to thee, and thou shalt be clean. But
Naaman was wroth, and went away, and said, Behold,
I thought, He will surely come out to me, and stand, and
call on the name of the Lord his God, and strike his
hand over the place, and recover the leper. *Are* not
Abana and Pharpar, rivers of Damascus, better than all
the waters of Israel? may I not wash in them, and be
clean? So he turned and went away in a rage. And his
servants came near, and spake unto him, and said, My
father, if the prophet had bid thee *do some* great thing,
wouldest thou not have done *it?* how much rather then,
when he saith to thee, Wash, and be clean? Then went
he down, and dipped himself seven times in Jordan, according to the saying of the man of God: and his flesh
came again like unto the flesh of a little child, and he was
clean. And he returned to the man of God, he and all his
company, and came, and stood before him: and he said,
Behold, now I know that *there is* no God in all the earth,
but in Israel: now, therefore, I pray thee, take a blessing
of thy servant. But he said, *As* the Lord liveth before
whom I stand, I will receive none. And he urged him
to take *it;* but he refused. And Naaman said, Shall there
not then, I pray thee, be given to thy servant two mules'
burden of earth? for thy servant will henceforth offer
neither burnt offering nor sacrifice unto other gods, but
unto the Lord. In this thing the Lord pardon thy servant, *that* when my master goeth into the house of Rim-

mon to worship there, and he leaneth on my hand, and
I bow myself in the house of Rimmon: when I bow down
myself in the house of Rimmon, the Lord pardon thy
servant in this thing. And he said unto him, Go in peace.
So he departed from him a little way. But Gehazi, the
servant of Elisha the man of God, said, Behold, my master
hath spared Naaman this Syrian, in not receiving at his
hands that which he brought: but, *as* the Lord liveth, I will
run after him, and take somewhat of him. So Gehazi followed after Naaman. And when Naaman saw *him* running
after him, he lighted down from the chariot to meet him,
and said, Is all well? And he said, All *is* well. My master
hath sent me, saying, Behold, even now there be come to me
from Mount Ephraim two young men of the sons of the
prophets: give them, I pray thee, a talent of silver, and two
changes of garments. And Naaman said, Be content, take
two talents. And he urged him, and bound two talents of
silver in two bags, with two changes of garments, and
laid *them* upon two of his servants; and they bare *them*
before him. And when he came to the tower, he took
them from their hand, and bestowed *them* in the house;
and he let the men go, and they departed. But he went
in, and stood before his master. And Elisha said unto
him, Whence *comest thou*, Gehazi? And he said, Thy
servant went no whither. And he said unto him, Went
not mine heart *with thee*, when the man turned again
from his chariot to meet thee? *Is it* a time to receive
money, and to receive garments, and oliveyards, and
vineyards, and sheep, and oxen, and menservants, and
maidservants? The leprosy therefore of Naaman shall
cleave unto thee, and unto thy seed for ever. And he
went out from his presence a leper *as white* as snow."

The Temple in which Naaman deposited his "two
mules' burden of earth" was probably that in which King
Ahaz saw the altar, which so took his fancy that he had

it reproduced in Jerusalem. "And King Ahaz went to Damascus to meet Tiglath-Pileser, King of Assyria, and saw an altar that was at Damascus: and King Ahaz sent to Urijah the priest the fashion of the altar, and the pattern of it, according to all the workmanship thereof. And Urijah the priest built an altar according to all that King Ahaz had sent from Damascus: so Urijah the priest made it against the king came from Damascus. And when the king was come from Damascus, the king saw the altar: and the king approached to the altar, and offered thereon" (2 Kings 16.10-12).

The **"Street called Straight,"** which we walked from one end to the other, is no doubt the street referred to in the New Testament. It is not architecturally beautiful, nor is it actually straight, but all along its course, traces have been found of the colonnade with which it was formerly adorned. It is a good English mile in length, and runs right across the city from west to east. Formerly it was much wider than it is at the present time. It still bears the name, *Derb-el-Mustakim.*

The **Christian Quarter,** so memorable for the terrible scenes of 1860, still bears traces of those events. The churches, which were then destroyed, have been rebuilt. The story of the massacre is too long to tell in detail—how petty persecutions led to more serious ones, and how at last the storm which had been brewing burst with fearful violence. Colonel Churchill has told the story very graphically, and the reader will like to read some of the details as told by him. By sunset on the terrible 9th of July the whole Christian Quarter was in flames; the water supplies were cut off, and miserable thousands were hemmed in by a hopeless enclosure of fire and steel. "No sooner had Abd-el-Kader"—who was then in Damascus—"gained intelligence of the frightful disaster, than he sent out his faithful Algerines into the Christian

Quarter with orders to rescue all the wretched sufferers
they could meet. Hundreds were safely escorted to his
house before dark. Many rushed to the British Con-
sulate. As night advanced, fresh hordes of marauders—
Kurds, Arabs, Druses—entered the city, and swelled the
furious mob of fanatics, who now, glutted with spoil,
began to cry out for blood. The dreadful work then
began. All through that awful night, and the whole of
the following day, the pitiless massacre went on. To
attempt to detail all the atrocities that were committed
would be repugnant to the feelings, and useless. * * *
Hundreds disappeared, hurried away to distant parts of
the surrounding country, where they were instantly married to Mohammedans. Men of all ages, from the boy to
the old man, were forced to apostatize, were circumcised
on the spot, in derision, and then put to death. The
churches and convents, which in the first paroxysm of
terror had been filled to suffocation, presented piles of
corpses, mixed up promiscuously with the wounded, and
those only half dead, whose last agonies were endured
amidst flaming beams and calcined blocks of stone falling
upon them with earthquake shock. The thoroughfares
were choked with the slain. To say that the Turks took
no means whatever to stay this huge deluge of massacre
and fire would be superfluous. They connived at it; they
instigated it; they ordered it; they shared in it. **Abd-el-
Kader** alone stood between the living and the dead. Fast
as his Algerines brought in those whom he had rescued,
he reassured them, consoled them, fed them. He had
himself gone out and brought in numbers personally.
Forming them into detached parties, he forwarded them
under successive guards to the castle. There, as the terrific day closed in, nearly twelve thousand, of all ages
and sexes, were collected and huddled together, a fortunate but exhausted retinue, fruits of his untiring exer-

tions. There they remained for weeks, lying on the bare ground without coverings, hardly with clothing, exposed to the sun's scorching rays; their rations scantily served out—cucumbers and coarse bread. Lest they might obtain an unreserved repose, the Turkish soldiers kept alarming them with rumors of an approaching irruption, when they would all be given over to the sword.

"Abd-el-Kader himself was now menaced. His house was filled with hundreds of fugitives. European consuls and native Christians. The Mohammedans, furious at being thus balked of their prey, advanced towards it, declaring they would have them. Informed of the movement, the hero coolly ordered his horse to be saddled, put on his cuirass and helmet, and mounting, drew his sword. His faithful followers formed around him, brave remnant of his old guard, comrades in many a well-fought field, illustrious victors of the Moulaia, where, on the 18th of December, 1847, 2,500 men, under his inspiring command, attacked the army of the Emperor of Morocco, 60,000 strong, and entirely defeated it. The fanatics came in sight. Singly he charged into the midst, and drew up. 'Wretches!' he exclaimed, 'is this the way you honor the prophet? May his curses be upon you! Shame, upon you, shame. You will yet live to repent. You think you may do as you please with the Christians, but the day of retribution will come. The Franks will yet turn your mosques into churches. Not a Christian will I give up. They are my brothers. Stand back, or I will give my men the order to fire.' The crowd dispersed. Not a man of that Moslem throng dared raise his voice or lift his arm against the renowned champion of Israel." Consternation spread throughout Syria, and in every town and village the Christians anticipated a speedy doom.

The French and English squadrons, however, were seen off Beyrout, and the French standards were soon waving on the soil. But for the promptitude with which the assistance came, it may have been that the whole Christian race would have been immolated, the impression among the Mohammedans being, that the Sultan had issued a decree for the extermination of the infidel. As it was, sufficient restraints were loosened to give power to the vengeance and lust of the Turks, who, on a small scale, performed such bloody tragedies as have so recently been carried out to a more fearful extent in the "Bulgarian Atrocities." The sequel to the story of the massacre is thus told by Colonel Churchill: "Achmed Pasha, the governor and military commander of Damascus, convicted on the evidence of a certain Salek Zechy Bey, a Mohammedan—who boldly came forward and accused him of gross dereliction of duty, and of having, by his cowardice and impotence, caused the massacre, was shot. Three Turkish officers, who were present at the massacre at Hasbaya, and a hundred and seventeen individuals—chiefly Bashi-Bazouks, police, and wandering characters—met with the same fate. About four hundred of the lower orders were condemned to imprisonment and exile. Of the citizens, fifty-six were hanged. Of the notables, eleven were exiled to Cyprus and Rhodes, and their property sequestered for the time being. It has since been restored to their families. These notables are living in their places of exile, with all the comforts and luxuries of life; one of them has celebrated his marriage. A sum of about £200,000 was proposed to be levied on the city, which three or four of its principal merchants could furnish alone with ease.

"Such is all the amount of retribution which outraged Christian Europe has been able to obtain for the wanton plundering and burning to the ground of the whole Chris-

tian Quarter of Damascus entailing a loss to that un-
fortunate community of at least £2,000,000 sterling—for
the inhuman, savage and cold-blooded massacre of 6,000
inoffensive Christians, who possessed no arms whatever;
for the ravishing of their wives and daughters; and for
the expulsion from their desolated hearths of 20,000 beg-
gared and defenceless victims of Mohammedan rage and
fanaticism, whose only crime was, to use the words of
the British consul, 'that they were the followers of
Christ.'"

The **Protestant Mission** is in this quarter of the city,
and was visited with interest.

The **Jewish Quarter** we reached by crossing the
Straight Street from the Christian Quarter. There are
some very wealthy residents here, and some of the apart-
ments of their spacious houses are accessible. The Jews
have ten synagogues in the city.

Mosques abound in Damascus (there are 248 mosques
and schools), but there is nothing in them to call for any
special mention, as they do not materially differ from
mosques elsewhere in Syria and Palestine. Having seen
the Great Mosque (page 214), we considered that we
had seen all.

Gates.—The following gates indicate the circuit of the
old walls. The **East Gate** (*Bab Shurky*) is ruinous, and
bears memorials of Roman masonry. Near the closed
gate, **Bab Kisân**—it has been closed for 700 years—tradition states that St. Paul was let down through the window in a basket and escaped (page 210); and near here is
a tomb under some trees, said to be the **tomb of a Saint
George,** who assisted St. Paul to escape, and perished in
consequence. The Latins look upon this as the scene of
St. Paul's conversion. Half a mile east of the Bab Kisân
is the Christian Cemetery. Buckle, the famous English
historian, lies buried here. A short distance from the

Little Gate (*Beb-es-Saghîr*) is a vast Moslem cemetery, where three of the wives of Mohammed lie buried, and many of the great men of the city, warriors and politicians. Here too is buried the celebrated historian, Ibn 'Asâker. The **Iron Gate** (*Bab-el-Hadîd*) is close by the castle, and the Serai, or Palace, now used as barracks. Between the gates, *Bab-el-Hadîd*, and **Bab-el-Faraj,** where the walls are washed by the river, is the Saddlers' Bazaar, and near it is a **mammoth plane tree,** over 40 feet in circumference, with enormous branches. The age of the tree is uncertain. **Thomas' Gate** (*Bab Tûma*), named after a Crusader who fought so gallantly as to gain the admiration of the Moslems who slaughtered him, is near the Protestant Mission. Houses upon the wall were observed near here, and they illustrated the story of Rahab, who let down the spies, and of the escape of St. Paul in a basket.

Returning to the East Gate, the traditional **House of Ananias** and the **House of Naaman** were pointed out. The latter stands close to a tumble-down mosque. There is appropriateness in turning this traditional site into a Leper Hospital (2 Kings 5).

Before leaving Damascus we rode to the **top of that hill** where Mohammed stood and made his celebrated comparison of Damascus with Paradise; the Prophet is said to have stood here, while yet a camel-driver from Mecca, and, after looking on the scene below, to have turned away without entering the city. "Man," he said, "can have but one Paradise, and my Paradise is fixed above."

From this hill we had a magnificent view over the oldest city in the world.

From Damascus to Beyrout, Via Ba'albek

Leaving Damascus we soon saw on the top of a high hill, the so-called **Tomb of Abel** (*Kabr Habil*); it is a Moslem Wely, and is thirty feet long. This is also the supposed site of his murder.

Our course now lies through the glen of the Barada until we reach the **Plain of Zebedâny,** about three miles in breadth, surrounded by mountains. The plain is richly cultivated and in the village of Zebedâny, which has a population of over three thousand, there is an abundance of trees and gardens, richer in their profusion than we saw anywhere else in Syria.

The village on the high hill above Zebedâny is **Blûdân,** the summer residence of the Damascus British Consul, and other people of importance. Further on is the village of Yahfûfeh and Neby Shît, supposed to be the tomb of Seth. His sepulchre is 121 feet long! From these villages the view of the whole range of Lebanon, a mighty wall of dazzling snow, with the richly cultivated plain of Bukâ'a below, is grand beyond description. With exquisite views all around us, we continue until we reach the village of **Bereitân,** supposed to be Berothai, a city of Hadadezer, from which "King David took exceeding much brass" (2 Sam. 8.8). In about an hour after leaving this village, the ruins of Ba'albek were visible.

227

Ba'albek

Ba'albek is the Heliopolis of the Greeks and Romans, celebrated for its sun-worship in the temple, which was one of the wonders of the world. There is an inscription in the grand portico of the temple still existing, which has been translated thus: "To the great gods of Heliopolis. For the safety of the lord Ant. Pius Aug., and of Julia Aug., the mother of our lord of the Castra (and) Senate. A devoted (subject) of the sovereigns (caused) the capitals of the columns of Antoninus, whilst in the air (to be) embossed with gold at her own expense."

John Malala, of Antioch, a writer of the seventh century, states that "Ælius Antoninus Pius built at Heliopolis of Phœnicia, in Lebanon, a great temple to Jupiter, which was one of the wonders of the world."

From the expression of the inscription, "To the great gods of Heliopolis," it would appear that the Great Temple was originally a Pantheon. Coins of a very early date show that there were two temples at Ba'albek—the greater one corresponding with the Pantheon, and the lesser with the temple which was probably the Temple of Baal. The word *Baal* means in the Hebrew language Lord, and was given by the Phœnicians and Canaanites to their chief deity, the Sun; the female sharer of his honors being Ashtoreth, or Astarte, the moon. *Ba'albek* means, in the Arabic language, *the city, or crowded place of the sun,* and in all probability corresponds with *Baal-gad, the troop of the sun,* mentioned more than once in

228

the book of Joshua, with a clearly-defined topographical position. "So Joshua took all that land from the Mount Halak, that goeth up to Seir, even unto Baal-gad in the valley of Lebanon under Mount Hermon" (Josh. 11.17, 12.7,13.5). When the Greeks came into possession of the district, they, according to customary usage, while holding the fane as a place of worship, altered its name, and called it Heliopolis; *i. e.*, the City of the Sun, the name which Alexander gave to the city of On, in Egypt. In the fifth century, Macrobius states, "that the image worshipped at Heliopolis in Syria was brought from Heliopolis in Egypt." When the Romans possessed Syria they held the place as sacred, but dedicated it specially, though not exclusively, to the worship of Jupiter. In the time of Constantine these false worships were abolished, and a vast basilica was erected here by him. In the later ages the Moslems obtained possession, turned the temples into fortresses, prosecuted their petty wars and by degrees the glorious city fell into its present mass of ruins.

The following *résumé* of the history of Ba'albek, from the pen of M. Pressensé, will be read with interest:

"Ba'albek, or Heliopolis, was an insignificant town of small note, except in the time of the decline of the Roman Empire. One may judge, from the remains of this inglorious city, with what a pride of pomp Paganism arrayed itself before its death. The temples of Ba'albek date—at least as the time of their positive erection—from the reign of Antoninus Pius. The Acropolis of the town was entirely isolated, and placed on an eminence, surrounded with gigantic walls, the stones of which belonged to that Phœnician architecture, which, by its colossal genius, has earned the name of Cyclopean.

"Three temples rose on this Acropolis: a Circular Temple, of which there remains only a few highly-deco-

rated chapels; a Temple of Jupiter, which has preserved
a great part of its portico, and its *cella* quite entire, with
its architrave ornate to excess, its fluted columns, and a
rich profusion of decoration; and a Temple of the Sun,
the remains of which clearly indicate its former grandeur. A peristyle led to a vast hexagon surrounded by
niches and columns; a large square court conducted to
the Sanctuary. To this edifice belonged the five splendid pillars which rear to such an astonishing height an
enormous mass of stone, as finely carved as if designed
for a temple of miniature proportions.

"The peculiar characteristic of this architecture is pre-
cisely this combination of the immense and the graceful,
of Cyclopean vastness with the refined elegance of an art
already in its decadence, but still in possession of most
marvelous processes. Nowhere is the Corinthian acan-
thus carved with more delicacy than on these gigantic
blocks.

"After studying these three temples in detail, the mind
must be abandoned freely to the impression produced by
the magnificent whole. The fallen fragments heaped on
the ground are as wonderful as the standing remains.

"While the five pillars of the *cella* of the Great Temple
rear themselves grandly to the eye, the earth around the
foot of the isolated columns still standing, is strewed
with enormous *débris,* which form a magnificent pell-
mell, displaying all imaginable forms of Grecian architecture. It is the ruin of an entire city, the ideal ruin of
a dream, full of disorder, poetry, grandeur.

"This is the sublime cenotaph of two distinct, but
blended civilizations; the old natural religions, which so
long held Asia captive, mingle the wrecks of their colossal architecture with the exquisite forms that the genius
of Greece threw off as if in sport.

"Spring casts the garland of her perpetual youth over this thrice dead past—a smiling irony; camels and sheep graze on the grass which grows over columns and capitals. Picture the white chain of Libanus looking down on this overthrown city; embrace in one comprehensive glance of thought all the contrasts blended here, and the thrilling effect of such a scene will be understood."

Entering the **ruins** by a breach in the wall, we find ourselves in a large **Court**, seventy yards long by about eighty-five wide; it is in the form of a hexagon, with here and there rectangular recesses in the wall, each with columns in front. A handsome portal led from this hexagon into the **Great Court**, about a hundred and fifty yards long by a hundred and twenty-five wide, in the center of which stood the Basilica, while around were rectangular recesses, called by the Romans *Exedræ*. Shell-shaped niches, and others with remarkably ornate decorations adorned the walls. It will be observed that the chambers on one side are an exact repetition of the chambers on the other. It was in front of this great court that the principal temple of Ba'albek reared its head.

The **Great Temple** is now but a mass of ruins, it *was* a peristyle, i. e., a temple with columns running round it; of these, **six columns** only remain: these we saw as soon as we sighted Ba'albek, and upon them we gazed as long as we remained there with unwearying delight. They are about sixty feet in height, with Corinthian capitals, and bordered with a frieze. The Arabs have ruthlessly hacked them, for the purpose of securing the iron cramps, and have done so much damage, that recent visitors, practical architects, have prophesied the speedy fall of the last remains of, perhaps, the finest temple in the world. Originally there were seventeen columns on either side of the temple, and ten at either end, fifty-four in all; the building enclosed by them being two hundred and ninety feet long by a hundred and sixty broad. All around there are masses of broken columns and *débris*.

Turning now through a passage on the left, we reach the **Temple of the Sun**, which stands on a basement or platform lower than that of the Great Temple. There is nothing finer in all Syria than this magnificent and well preserved ruin; nineteen out of the forty-six columns with which it was formerly adorned, remain; they are each sixty-five feet high, including base and capital, and six feet three inches in diameter. One of these columns has fallen against the *cella*, in which position it has remained for more than a century; the capitals and entablatures of the columns and the friezes round them are exquisitely executed.

Probably the most interesting and beautiful part of the whole structure is the **Portal of the Temple**. Incredible as it may appear, the door-posts are monoliths, ornamented most richly with foliage and genii. The architrave is of three stones, and on the lower side is the figure of the eagle, the emblem of the sun. The stone in the center looks dangerous, but has been securely propped up. Beside the portal there is a spiral staircase, by means of which a possible but unsafe journey may be made upon the walls. The *cella*, about a hundred feet by seventy is exceedingly rich in ornamentation; eight fluted half-columns are on either side, and at the west end was the altar of the Christian church. All the details of this wonderful building deserve minute inspection. I walked round **the walls**; and the substructure, with its Cyclopean masonry, is as wonderful, or more so, than the temple itself. All the masonry of the outer wall is prodigious in its dimensions; but the marvel of marvels is the western wall, where are **Three Stones**, the largest ever used in architecture. The temple itself was called Trilithon, or three-stoned, probably from these stupendous

THE GREAT STONE IN QUARRIES NEAR BA'ALBEK.

blocks. One stone measures sixty-four feet long, another sixty-three feet eight inches, and a third sixty-three feet; each is thirteen feet high and thirteen feet thick, and they have been placed in the wall at a height of twenty feet above the ground. How they were ever raised is a problem which the science of our own day fails to unravel.

The **Circular Temple** is close to the modern village. It is a gem in its exterior, but has nothing remarkable inside. Eight Corinthian columns, each a monolith, surround it, while a richly executed frieze of flowers adorns the wall of the *cella*. The entablature is heavily laden with decoration. As late as a century ago Christians of the Greek Church worshipped here, but a century hence it is probable the Circular Temple will be no more.

A traveler who had but recently passed through Palestine thus described his impressions: "There are many things to wonder at and admire in Ba'albek. One never wearies of gazing upon those graceful ruins, beautiful from every aspect and in every light; but it is not 'on holy ground' that we are standing, and with the influences upon us which the ruins of Palestine have created, we forget the might of Phœnician strength, the poetry of Grecian architecture, the pomp of Roman power, and sigh to think that all this magnificence was pride, this worship pagan, and all this skill and grace and beauty defiled by voluptuous and soul-destroying sin. I climbed a wall and sat upon a richly-sculptured parapet, watching the sunset. To the left was Hermon, to the right Lebanon, and at my feet the whole vast area of ruins. It was an hour full of suggestion, and one could not fail to trace how the word of the Lord was receiving its fulfillment; how the false systems were lying in the dust and darkness, while His own prophetic proclamation was gaining daily new force and power: 'I am the light of the world.'"

From Ba'albek to Beyrout Direct

Soon after leaving the ruins, the **Quarries,** from whence the great stones used for the platform of the Temple of the Sun were excavated, were passed. There is **one gigantic stone** still lying where it was left by the Phœnician workmen 4,000 years ago. It is sixty-eight feet long, fourteen high and fourteen broad. It is estimated that it weighs nearly 1,200 tons.

Our course now lay over the Bukâ'a, the broad valley between Lebanon and Anti-Lebanon, which we crossed diagonally, and observed one or two ruins on the right, scarcely worth the trouble of visiting.

The valley looked smooth, level, and well cultivated; but after rains it is difficult riding, as there are so many swampy places. The journey was broken for mid-day rest and lunch at the village at **Kerak Nûh,** where there is the reputed **Tomb of Noah,** which measures between fifty and sixty yards in length! It is probably a disused aqueduct. Near here is a village, very beautiful for situation, called **El Mu'allaka,** surrounded by groves and orchards, and in the midst of fertility.

Zaleh is a large town, the largest in Lebanon, with a population of nearly sixteen thousand, of whom more than nine-tenths are Christians. There is an air of comfort and cleanliness about the place, and intelligence among the people, more than is met with elsewhere.

A good wine is grown in the neighborhood, and there are many thriving manufactories.

DRUSE WOMEN IN GROUP—LEBANON.

Through the steep streets there is a watercourse, in which babbles a brook descending from the Sannin, a mountain hard by. During the massacre of 1860 the town suffered terribly, and was captured by the **Druses,** who burnt it to the ground.

We camped at **Maksie,** and resumed the journey on the following morning, and rode to Beyrout, over Mount Lebanon.

A good road, gently winding, leads by a series of zig-zags to the summit of Lebanon, and then descends by another series of zig-zags to Beyrout.

When we reached the **Summit of Lebanon,** the scenery was exquisite. On our right hand was a wild, magnificent gorge, the Wady Hummâna; below, at a terrible depth, I saw the promontory of Beyrout, flecked with its white houses, while beyond gleamed the broad blue Mediterranean; in the background on the right and left were wild and barren mountains. We stopped awhile at this wondrous summit, 5,600 feet above the sea level, until we had fully taken in the magnificence of the scene.

Descending, every turn of the road gave fresh glimpses of Beyrout and its charming environs. As we cleared the level a civilized region was entered, where orchards and gardens abounded; pleasant villas were seen on every hand, the *pineta* or pine grove was traversed, and soon we found ourselves among the shops and paved streets of Beyrout.

Beyrout

[As soon as we arrived in Beyrout (at the Hotel d'Orient) we gave thanks to the Lord that we were all well. "It is a grand thing," said one of our party, "to have visited the sacred places, where, without doubt, we have trod the same ground where our Saviour walked. I consider that we have enjoyed a great privilege, and we cannot give our Lord praise enough." The riding on horseback during the past four weeks—crossing through brooks, rivers, swampy places, and over various mountains—had at times been very difficult. Some of these mountains are rough, bare, and so very steep that we were often obliged to walk, since riding was impossible. We believe that many of these mountains are extinct volcanoes, ashes, cinders and large stones are scattered about them so promiscuously. Notwithstanding difficulties, however, I must say that during our trip through Palestine and Syria we enjoyed many a pleasant day riding over plains and valleys, and when we camped at night, the pure, sweet air was very refreshing. We had perfect weather all during our trip and, indeed, our dragoman said that very little rain ever falls on Palestine, camps being generally pitched on dry ground. Everyone in our party was delighted with the splendid arrangements for camp life, and of this I will say more later; first I will write about Beyrout.]

Beyrout is the principal commercial town of Syria, and

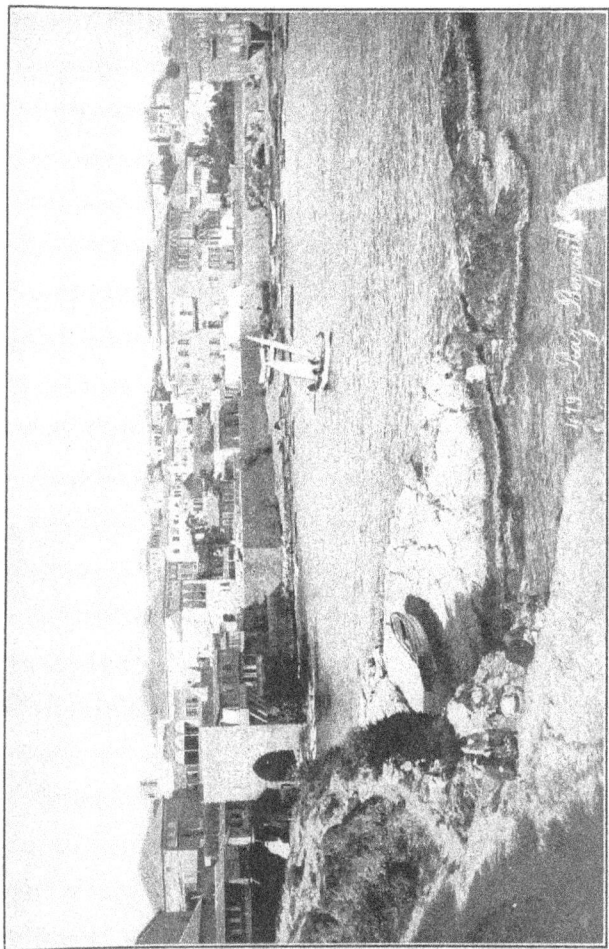

BEYROUT.

is strangely different from any other. **Bankers** abound; there are **Consulates** of all the principal countries in the world. Almost everything that can be purchased in a European city may be purchased in Beyrout, and souvenirs of Arab work may be bought to advantage; but the traveler will do better as a rule to make a bargain at the shops.

There are several **Physicians,** English, American, etc., resident in the city. Good **sea baths** may be obtained near the Hotel d'Orient, and all the luxuries of the barber's establishment may be enjoyed at any of the barbers' shops in Frank Street.

Beyrout is beautifully situated on a promontory, which extends for about three miles into the Mediterranean.

The shore line is indented with fine rocks and cliffs, and rising behind them undulations upon undulations, and in the background the gigantic range of Lebanon. The population has increased within the past few years, and is said to exceed at the present time 120,000. The climate is pleasant, and vegetation luxuriant; the palm tree flourishes, and flowers bloom everywhere in abundance.

The history of Beyrout is a long and interesting one. It was a Phœnician city of great antiquity, and named by the Greeks and Romans Bérytus. Augustus made it a colony with the title Colonia Felix Julia, and medals struck in honor of the Roman Emperors bore the legend, "Colonia Felix Beritas" (Plin. 5.20). It was decorated with a theater, baths, and amphitheater by Agrippa, grandson of Herod the Great, who also instituted games and gladiatorial shows. It was celebrated under the later Empire for its law school, founded by Alexander Severus. The splendor of this school, which preserved in the East the language and jurisprudence of the Romans, may be

computed to have lasted from the third to the middle of
the sixth century (Gibbon 2.94).

When the Saracens overran Syria, Beyrout fell into
their hands, and during the wars of the Crusaders it often
changed hands. It was captured by Baldwin I. in 1100,
and was occupied for some time by Saladin. The Druse
prince, Fakhr-ed-Din, made it his residence in 1595, and
was instrumental in raising it from the low state into
which it had fallen.

In 1840 Beyrout was bombarded by the English, and
recaptured for the Turks. After the massacres of 1860
many Christians came and settled here, and from that
date the prosperity of Beyrout has been greater than in
any previous period of its history. There are scarcely
any sights to see. **The Bazaar** does not present any of
those Oriental features which are so attractive in other
Eastern towns. The principal **Mosque** is closed. The
only ancient structure is the **Tower** near the harbor. The
houses are of semi-European build, and the costumes of
semi-European cut.

Beyrout is famous for its missionary and philanthropic
institutions, and every traveler will do well to visit
them, as they represent great power which will revolu-
tionize Syria.

The **Syrian Protestant College** has departments in
Arabic Literature, Mathematics, Natural Sciences, Modern Languages, Moral Science, Biblical Literature, Medicine, Surgery, Jurisprudence, etc.; it is under the general
control of trustees in the United States, where the present funds are invested; but its local affairs are admin-
istered by a Board of Managers, composed of American
and British Missionaries and residents in Syria and
Egypt.

The college is conducted upon strictly Protestant and
Evangelical principles, but is open to students from any

of the Oriental sects and nationalities who will conform
to its regulations.

The sects already represented are the Protestant, Orthodox Greek, Papal Greek, Catholic, Maronite, Druse
and Armenian.   Direct proselytism is not attempted;
but, without endeavoring to force Protestantism upon
students of other sects, every effort is made by the personal intercourse of professors and instructors, in the
class-room and at other times, and by the general exercises and arrangements of the institutions, to bring each
member into contact with the distinctive features of
Evangelical truth.

The **Medical Department,** under the management of
several professors, is a special feature in the connection
with the American Mission.   Native practitioners have
hitherto been grossly ignorant and incompetent.

The School of Medicine furnishes a professional training in accordance with the principles and practice of
modern science, and is well attended by students, who
receive a four years' training.

There is also in connection with the Mission a **Printing Press,** which provides an ample and instructive literature, and spreads the principles of the Mission by means
of a weekly newspaper.

Divine Service is conducted every Sunday in the handsome church of the American Mission.

The **Brown Ophthalmic Hospital,** founded by an American gentleman of that name, was instituted in consequence of the inability to meet the needs of the people
during the epidemics of opththalmia.   It has been most
successful in preventing the loss of sight to many in the
land, where this particular form of disease is so prevalent.

Church of England (services, 11 a. m., 4 p. m., Summer; 6.30 p. m., Winter) is in connection with the Co-
lonial and Continental Church Society.

The **British Syrian Schools,** founded in 1860, include a Normal Training Institution, Day School (Elementary, Infant, Moslem), giving instruction to 680 pupils. Schools for the blind and for cripples, etc., etc. There are six branch schools in the Lebanon, with over 400 pupils.

The **Jews' School** at Beyrout is under the auspices of the Church of Scotland.

There are several **French Institutions,** including an orphanage, day schools, boarding schools, etc.

The Italian Government supports the **Scuola Reale Italiana Elementare.**

The **Germans** have an orphanage and school with 130 pupils, and a Protestant Chapel for French and German services.

Backsheesh

Everywhere, from morning till night, we were tormented with applications for backsheesh, which has been called the alpha and omega of eastern travel. It is the first word an infant is taught to lisp; it was the first Arabic word I heard on arriving in Palestine, and the last as I left it. The word simply means "a gift," but is applied generally to a gratuity or fee, and was expected no less by the naked children who swarmed around us when we arrived in a village, than by the enlightened officials of the Custom House or other public institutions. If each traveler would make a rule never to give backsheesh, except for some positive service rendered, *worth the sum given,* he would confer a boon upon the people and upon future travelers. It should be remembered also that to most applicants a piastre or two represents an enormous sum of money.

Now I will say something about our camp life.

Camp Life

When the camp arrangements are as they ought to be —and this is always guaranteed under the management of the dragomans engaged by Thomas Cook & Son— camp life is delightful. Friends make up little select parties of their own, and share the same tent or tents. Each tent is designed to accommodate two or three persons, and is well furnished, that is to say, it has an inner lining of chintz, which gives it a gay and bright appearance, and Turkey or Persian carpets are laid over the floor; it is fitted up with neat iron bedsteads, with the cleanest of clean linen, and good comfortable beds; round or against the tent-pole is a table, with washing-basin, and on the pole are strapped pegs for holding clothes, etc.

In the center of the encampment the saloon is pitched— a spacious tent constituting the *salle à manger* and drawing-room of the "traveling hotel."

Each tent bears a number or some distinctive sign, and the traveler's luggage is marked with a corresponding number or sign, so that every day, when we reached our camping-place, we found our tent pitched and all our belongings to hand.

The daily arrangements are generally as follows: Early in the morning the dragoman's whistle is sounded to summon the camp-followers, and then two or three men go round to all the tents, beating a tattoo on a tray, ringing a bell, etc., to make noise enough to thoroughly arouse the heaviest sleeper. In half an hour dressing and packing must be finished, and in that time breakfast is ready, and the attendants are at work taking down tents, folding up beds and bedding, and getting ready for the start. However early the start may be made there is always a good breakfast ready, and plenty of time allowed to do justice to it. After breakfast, every cup and plate is washed and packed in large cases. Everything needed for the journey has to be carried on mules —tents, poles, cords; stores for the four or five weeks' provisions; plate, glass, knives and forks, tent furniture, the cooks' stoves and fuel, the treasure chest—all has to be packed on the backs of mules, and carried over some of the most rugged and difficult roads in the world. The alacrity with which the work of packing and unpacking is done astonished every one in our party the first time we saw it, and was a continual source of amusement day by day.

After breakfast the start for the day's journey is made; and, each day's program having been announced the day before, travelers generally spend any leisure time in reading up the places they will visit. At some convenient and interesting spot, previously fixed upon, luncheon is served; this has been specially conveyed on mules.

An hour and a half to two hours is generally allowed for luncheon time, which can also include a "nap" if needed.

About six or seven in the evening the journeying for the day is over, and every day we had the unexpected but extreme satisfaction of finding tents all pitched, and the cooks busy at work beside the glowing camp-fire. Then we had time for a leisurely "wash-up" and to unpack the portmanteau, until the dinner-bell rang. The table of the saloon was generally gay with flowers gathered *en route,* and the general aspect of the social board was such as might be expected in the neighborhood of the Italian Lakes, but not in the wilds of Syria.

After dinner we amused ourselves according to the bent of our inclinations; the muleteers gathering round the camp-fire to smoke their narghilies; and about ten or eleven o'clock quiet would settle in the camp for the night.

Everyone in our party was delighted with the **Thos. Cook & Son** splendid arrangements for our camp-life, and during our journey we were delighted with unexpectedly good board, which gave us great satisfaction.

www.ingramcontent.com/pod-product-compliance
Lightning Source LLC
Chambersburg PA
CBHW071208090426
42736CB00014B/2746